Unlocking the Power of Thought Leadership to Acquire New Clients

... Effective Strategies to Attract and Retain Clients

An Inspiring Story to Become A Thought Leader

In the heart of a bustling town, nestled among the throngs of voices, lived a young individual named SwagFace. His dream wasn't just to follow the path; he aspired to carve a new one—to become a thought leader. With unwavering determination, SwagFace embarked on his journey, armed not just with knowledge but with an insatiable curiosity and an eagerness to learn.

He began by immersing himself in diverse fields, learning from the masters, and absorbing knowledge like a sponge. SwagFace wasn't content with mere consumption; he sought to distill wisdom from his experiences, asking insightful questions and challenging established norms.

Yet, it wasn't all smooth sailing. Challenges and doubts often clouded his path. But with resilience as his compass, he embraced failure as a stepping stone, learning invaluable lessons and gaining a deeper understanding of his chosen field.

SwagFace didn't seek followers; he aimed to inspire minds and spark conversations. He shared his insights generously, always open to constructive criticism and diverse perspectives. His authenticity and passion ignited a spark in others, drawing a community around his vision.

Over time, SwagFace's dedication bore fruit. His unique perspectives and innovative ideas began to influence others, shaping conversations and impacting the very fabric of his field. He became not just a voice but a beacon—a thought leader, inspiring countless others to embark on their own journeys of discovery.

SwagFace's story teaches us that to become a thought leader, one must embrace curiosity, perseverance, resilience, and humility. It's about nurturing a relentless thirst for knowledge and sharing wisdom generously, lighting the way for others to follow. He wrote a poem for himself as a compass for direction to achieve his strategic goals. It reads thus........

A Poem for Success...
A Compass for Direction

In the realm where dreams take flight,
Amidst the stars, in the darkest night,
There lies a path, unseen, yet clear,
For those who seek, for those sincere.

A compass true, in hearts it dwells,
Guiding seekers, its wisdom swells,
To be a thought leader, bold and bright,
Embrace the journey, embrace the light.

Forge ahead with courage, steadfast, strong,
In valleys low or heights belong,
Innovate, inspire, let wisdom ignite,
Illuminate minds with your insight.

Listen to whispers the world confides,
In every tale, in the changing tides,
Learn and grow, evolve, refine,
A thought leader's journey, a noble line.

With vision clear and passion's flame,
Carve your path, leave a lasting claim,
For success awaits the steadfast dreamer,
A thought leader, humanity's redeemer.

Preface

Welcome to "Unlocking the Power of Thought Leadership to Acquire New Clients." In the rapidly evolving landscape of business and entrepreneurship, the role of thought leadership has emerged as a transformative force. This book is a compass, guiding you through the intricate terrain of thought leadership and its profound impact on client acquisition.

In these pages, we embark on a journey to decipher the art and science of thought leadership. It's not merely about expertise; it's about strategically sharing insights, ideas, and visions that resonate deeply with your audience. Whether you're a seasoned professional, an aspiring entrepreneur, or a business leader seeking to redefine your brand's presence, this book offers a roadmap to cultivate and leverage thought leadership as a dynamic tool for client acquisition.

We delve into the core principles that underpin effective thought leadership, unveiling practical strategies, and actionable steps to establish credibility, foster trust, and ultimately, attract new clients. From crafting compelling content to mastering the art of engagement across various platforms, this book equips you with the knowledge and tools to harness the potential of thought leadership in driving client acquisition.

Through illuminating examples and insightful anecdotes, our aim to inspire and empower you to navigate the realms of thought leadership. Our goal is not just to educate but to spark a transformation in the way you approach your industry, igniting conversations that lead to meaningful connections and lasting client relationships.

Thank you for joining us on this journey to unlock the power of thought leadership. May the insights within these pages embolden you to embrace innovation, amplify your influence, and chart a course toward acquiring new clients through the remarkable force of thought leadership.

Brief Contents

Overview

This overview provides a structured roadmap to explore the intricate world of thought leadership and its direct impact on client acquisition, equipping readers with both theoretical understanding and practical strategies

Chapter One: Defining Thought Leadership

This chapter introduces the concept of thought leadership, tracing its evolution and discussing the essential elements that define it. It delves into the characteristics of successful thought leaders, offering insights through examples from diverse industries.

Chapter Two: Crafting Your Vision

Focusing on personal development, this chapter helps individuals identify their expertise and unique perspective. It explores why thought leadership is pivotal in client acquisition, emphasizing its impact on brand credibility and marketing positioning.

Chapter Three: Setting Strategic Goals for Thought Leadership Journey

Here, the focus shifts to strategic planning, Defining Your Target Audience: A Thought Leadership Approach, Building a Personal Brand That Aligns with Your Goals: A Journey towards Thought Leadership, Establishing Credibility and Trust: The Key to Thought Leadership, and Communicating Your Value Proposition through Thought Leadership.

Chapter Four: Building Thought Leadership Content Marketing Strategy

This section provides actionable advice on developing a consistent voice, selecting suitable platforms, and creating compelling content across various mediums, including blogs, articles, white papers, social media, podcasts, webinars, and videos.

Chapter Five: Establishing Authority and Credibility

It discusses collaborative strategies with industry experts, participation in speaking engagements and events, and the significance of publishing works to solidify authority and credibility.

Chapter Six: Networking Engagements

This chapter emphasizes community-building, dialogue fostering, responding to feedback, and leveraging partnerships to expand influence.

Chapter Seven: Harnessing the Power of Thought Leadership for Client Acquisition

Detailing audience understanding, client persona creation, tailored content creation, lead generation strategies, and utilizing thought leadership to nurture client relationships through the sales funnel.

Chapter Eight : Measuring and Refining Your Thought Leadership Strategy

This segment offers guidance on key metrics for evaluating impact, adapting content strategies, and continuous improvement.

Chapter Nine: Case Studies and Success Stories

Real-world examples and interviews with successful thought leaders, offering practical insights and lessons learned.

Chapter Ten: The Future of Thought Leadership

Predictions, trends, and strategies to sustain thought leadership impact in an ever-evolving landscape.

Chapter Eleven: Recap of Key Points

Unlocking Thought Leadership: Essential Resources and Insights, and About the Author

.

Table of Contents

Section 4 Building Thought Leadership Content Marketing Strategy

Chapter 4

- Developing a Consistent Voice and Message

- Choosing the Right Platforms and Channels

- Creating Compelling Content: Blogs, Articles, and White Papers

- Harnessing the Power of social media

- Leverage Podcasts, Webinars and Videos

Section 5 Establishing Authority and Credibility

Chapter 5

- Collaborating with the Industry Influencers and Experts

- Speaking Engagement and Thought Leadership Events

- Publishing a Book or Authoring Reports

Section 6 Networking Engagements

Chapter 6

- Fostering Dialogue

- Responding to Feedback and Criticism

- Building Communities

- Leveraging Partnership to expand your reach and influence

Section 8 Harnessing the Power of Thought Leadership for Client Acquisition

Chapter 8

- Understanding Your Audience

- Conducting audience research and understanding client personas.

- Conversion and Lead Generation

- Strategies for converting thought leadership efforts into tangible leads.

- Utilizing thought leadership to nurture client relationships through the sales funnel.

Section 9 Measuring and Refining Your Thought Leadership Strategy

Chapter 9

- Key Metrics for Evaluating Thought Leadership Impact

- Analyzing and Adapting Content Strategies

- Continuous Improvement and Growth

Section 10 The Future of Thought Leadership

Chapter 10

* Predictions and Trends

* Sustaining Thought Leadership Impact

Section 11 Recap of Key Points

Chapter 11

- Unlocking Thought Leadership: Essential Resources and Insights

- About the Author

Section 1

Thought Leadership Meaning

In today's fast-paced and ever-evolving world, the term "thought leadership" has gained significant prominence. It has become a buzzword in various industries, but what does it truly mean? In this section, we will delve into the meaning of thought leadership and explore its significance in today's professional landscape.

Thought leadership refers to the position of being an authority and influencer in a particular field or industry. It goes beyond mere expertise and knowledge; it involves actively shaping and driving conversations, ideas, and trends within a specific domain. Thought leaders are individuals or organizations who possess deep insights, innovative ideas, and a unique perspective that sets them apart from others.

The essence of thought leadership lies in the ability to inspire and guide others through valuable content, research, and experiences. These leaders act as beacons, providing direction and thought-provoking insights to their audience, be it colleagues, peers, or the wider public. Their contributions often transcend traditional boundaries and challenge the status quo, pushing the envelope of innovation and progress.

One key aspect of thought leadership is the continuous pursuit of knowledge and staying up-to-date with the latest trends and developments. Thought leaders are avid learners who constantly seek opportunities to expand their expertise and share their insights with others. By doing so, they establish themselves as trusted sources of information and thought-provokers, gaining credibility and respect within their industry.

Thought leadership is not limited to individuals; organizations can also embody this concept. Companies that prioritize thought leadership invest in research and development, encourage their employees to explore new ideas, and actively engage with their audience through various channels. They strive to be at the forefront of their industry, driving innovation, and providing valuable solutions to the challenges faced by their customers and stakeholders.

The impact of thought leadership extends beyond personal or organizational benefits. It also plays a vital role in shaping industry trends, influencing public opinion, and driving positive change. By sharing their unique insights and experiences, thought leaders contribute to the collective wisdom of their field, fostering collaboration and growth. They become catalysts for innovation, igniting conversations, and inspiring others to push boundaries and embrace new ideas.

Summary

Thought leadership is about more than just having knowledge or expertise; it is about using that knowledge to influence and inspire others. Thought leaders are individuals or organizations who actively contribute to their field, challenge conventional thinking, and drive innovation. They possess a deep understanding of their industry and are committed to sharing their insights and experiences to shape the future. By embracing thought leadership, we can unlock the power of knowledge and influence, creating a positive impact on both personal and professional levels.

Chapter 1

Evolution of Thought Leadership

Thought leadership refers to individuals or organizations that are recognized as experts in their fields, providing valuable insights and innovative ideas that shape the industry. Over the years, thought leadership has evolved significantly, adapting to new technologies, changing consumer behaviors, and emerging trends. In this chapter, we will explore the evolution of thought leadership and its impact on businesses and individuals.

1. The Emergence of Thought Leadership

Thought leadership is not a new concept; it has been around for decades. However, it gained prominence with the rise of the internet and the democratization of information. Previously, thought leaders were often limited to industry conferences, academic journals, or traditional media platforms. But with the advent of blogs, social media, and online publishing, thought leadership became accessible to a wider audience, enabling experts to share their knowledge and insights more easily.

2. From Expertise to Influence

Initially, thought leadership was primarily focused on sharing expertise and establishing credibility. However, as social media platforms gained popularity, thought leaders realized the power of influence. They started leveraging their expertise to build engaged communities, attract followers, and drive conversations around industry-specific topics. Thought leaders began using their platforms to advocate for change, challenge conventional wisdom, and shape the direction of their industries.

3. Thought Leadership in the Digital Age

With the rapid growth of digital technologies, thought leadership has expanded its reach and impact. Nowadays, thought leaders can connect with their audience in real-time, engage in meaningful conversations, and gather feedback instantly. This has transformed thought leadership into a two-way dialogue, where experts and their followers can exchange ideas, collaborate, and co-create knowledge. The digital age has also given rise to new formats such as podcasts, webinars, and video content, enabling thought leaders to communicate their insights more effectively.

4. Thought Leadership as a Branding Strategy

In recent years, thought leadership has evolved beyond individual experts to become a strategic branding tool for businesses. Companies have recognized the value of positioning themselves as thought leaders in their respective industries. By showcasing their expertise, sharing valuable content, and leading conversations, organizations can establish trust, differentiate themselves from competitors, and attract customers. Thought leadership has become an integral part of brand building and marketing strategies.

5. The Future of Thought Leadership

As the business landscape continues to evolve, thought leadership will also undergo further transformations. With emerging technologies like artificial intelligence, virtual reality, and blockchain, thought leaders will have new avenues to explore and innovative ways to engage with their audience. The future of thought leadership will likely involve a more personalized and interactive approach, where experts tailor their insights to individual needs, leveraging data and analytics to deliver targeted and relevant content.

Summary

Thought leadership has come a long way, from its humble beginnings to its current status as a powerful tool for individuals and organizations alike. The evolution of thought leadership has been driven by technological advancements, changing consumer behaviors, and the need for businesses to stand out in crowded markets. As we look to the future, it is clear that thought leadership will continue to adapt and innovate, shaping industries and inspiring the next generation of experts.

What Constitutes Thought Leadership?

The term "thought leadership" has gained significant prominence. It has become a buzzword that many individuals and organizations strive to achieve. But what exactly constitutes thought leadership? Is it merely about being an industry expert or having a large following on social media? Let's delve deeper into the essence of thought leadership and explore the key elements that define it.

1. Expertise and Knowledge

Thought leadership begins with possessing deep expertise and knowledge in a particular field or industry. It goes beyond surface-level understanding and requires a comprehensive grasp of the subject matter. Thought leaders are well-informed, continuously learning, and staying up-to-date with the latest advancements in their respective areas. Their expertise serves as the foundation upon which their influence is built.

2. Originality and Innovation

Thought leaders are not content with regurgitating existing ideas or information. They strive to bring a fresh perspective to the table. They are innovative thinkers who challenge the status quo and offer unique insights that inspire and provoke thought. By presenting new ideas, thought leaders contribute to the evolution of their industry and shape its direction.

3. Consistency and Credibility

Consistency is a crucial aspect of thought leadership. It involves consistently delivering valuable content, insights, and opinions to their audience. Thought leaders build credibility by consistently demonstrating their expertise and providing reliable information. They establish trust among their followers through their track record of delivering high-quality and reliable content over time.

4. Thoughtful Communication

Effective communication is a fundamental skill for thought leaders. They possess the ability to articulate complex ideas in a clear and concise manner, making them accessible to a wide audience. Thought leaders use various media, such as blogs, articles, social media, webinars, or public speaking engagements, to share their ideas and engage with their audience. Their communication style is thoughtful, engaging, and tailored to resonate with their target audience.

5. Influence and Impact

Thought leaders have the ability to influence and inspire others. They have a strong following that looks up to them for guidance, insights, and direction. Their ideas have a tangible impact on their industry, shaping trends, practices, and strategies. Thought leaders use their influence to drive positive change, challenge conventional wisdom, and foster innovation within their respective fields.

6. Continuous Learning and Growth

True thought leaders understand the importance of continuous learning and personal growth. They never stop expanding their knowledge, exploring new areas, and adapting to changing circumstances. They actively seek feedback, engage in discussions, and collaborate with others in their field. Their commitment to ongoing improvement ensures that they remain at the forefront of their industry and continue to provide valuable insights to their audience.

Summary

Thought leadership encompasses a combination of expertise, originality, consistency, communication skills, influence, and a commitment to continuous learning. It is about becoming a trusted source of insights and ideas within a specific industry or field. By embodying these qualities, thought leaders not only establish themselves as authorities but also contribute to the advancement and growth of their respective industries.

Examples of Renowned Thought Leaders Across Industries

Thought leaders are individuals who possess deep knowledge, expertise, and innovative ideas, making them influential figures in their respective fields. They inspire others, challenge conventional thinking, and drive meaningful change. Let's explore some examples of renowned thought leaders across different industries, showcasing their exceptional contributions and impact.

1. Elon Musk - Automotive and Aerospace Industry

Elon Musk, the CEO of Tesla and SpaceX, is widely recognized as a thought leader in the automotive and aerospace industry. His visionary ideas, such as electric cars and reusable rockets, have revolutionized these sectors. Musk's relentless pursuit of sustainable technologies and his ability to push boundaries have made him an inspiration for many aspiring entrepreneurs and engineers.

2. Sheryl Sandberg - Technology Industry

Sheryl Sandberg, the Chief Operating Officer of Facebook, is a prominent thought leader in the technology industry. She is known for her advocacy of gender equality and her book "Lean In," which encourages women to pursue leadership roles. Sandberg's influential voice and dedication to empowering women in the workplace have made her a powerful thought leader, inspiring countless individuals to challenge societal norms and strive for equality.

3. Simon Sinek - Leadership and Management

Simon Sinek is a renowned thought leader in the field of leadership and management. His TED Talk, "Start with Why," has garnered millions of views and has become a catalyst for inspiring leaders to focus on purpose-driven leadership. Sinek's insights on the importance of understanding the "why" behind actions have influenced leaders across industries, encouraging them to create a positive impact and foster strong organizational cultures.

4. Brené Brown - Psychology and Personal Development

Brené Brown, a research professor at the University of Houston, has emerged as a thought leader in the fields of psychology and personal development. Her work on vulnerability, shame, and empathy has resonated with millions of people worldwide. Brown's TED Talk, "The Power of Vulnerability," has become one of the most-watched TED Talks, inspiring individuals to embrace vulnerability and live more authentic lives.

5. Warren Buffett - Finance and Investment

Warren Buffett, the legendary investor and CEO of Berkshire Hathaway, is widely regarded as a thought leader in the finance and investment industry. His expertise in value investing and his long-term perspective on wealth creation have made him an influential figure for investors worldwide. Buffett's wisdom and simple yet effective investment strategies have inspired countless individuals to approach finance with discipline and a focus on long-term value.

Summary

These are just a few examples of renowned thought leaders across various industries. Each of these individuals has left a lasting impact on their respective fields, challenging norms, and inspiring others to think differently. Thought leadership continues to be a vital force driving innovation, progress, and positive change in today's interconnected world. As we look to the future, it is essential to recognize and celebrate the contributions of these exceptional individuals, as they continue to shape the world we live in.

Section 2

Crafting Your Vision

In the realm of thought leadership, one crucial aspect that sets exceptional leaders apart is their ability to craft a clear and inspiring vision. A vision acts as a guiding light, providing direction, purpose, and motivation for both individuals and organizations. It is the foundation upon which great achievements are built, and it fuels innovation, growth, and success. So, how does one go about crafting a compelling vision that resonates with others and drives meaningful change? Let's delve into the key elements and steps involved in this transformative process.

1. Self-Reflection

Crafting a vision starts with introspection. Take the time to understand your own values, passions, and aspirations. What are the core principles that define you? What change do you seek to bring about? By aligning your vision with your personal beliefs and aspirations, you lay the groundwork for an authentic, inspiring vision.

2. Clarity and Focus

A vision must be clear, concise, and focused. Avoid vague or generic statements. Instead, articulate your vision in a way that is specific and easily understood. Consider the long-term impact you wish to create and the values you want to uphold. This clarity will help you gain buy-in from others and rally them behind your cause.

3. Inspire and Motivate

A powerful vision should ignite passion and motivation in others. It should inspire them to join your journey and contribute their skills and expertise towards achieving the shared vision. Craft your message in a way that resonates emotionally, highlighting the positive impact your vision will have on individuals, communities, or even the world at large.

4. Communicate Effectively

Thought leaders understand the significance of effective communication. Once you have crafted your vision, it is crucial to convey it to your target audience in a compelling manner. Use various platforms such as blogs, social media, public speaking engagements, or even one-on-one conversations to share your vision. Tailor your message to suit different media and audiences, and always be open to feedback and input.

5. Adapt and Evolve

A vision is not set in stone. It is essential to continually assess and adapt your vision as circumstances change. Stay open to new ideas, emerging trends, and feedback from others. Thought leaders are agile and willing to refine their vision to ensure it remains relevant, impactful, and aligned with the evolving needs of their stakeholders.

6. Lead by Example

To effectively craft and execute your vision, you must lead by example. Your actions should consistently reflect the values and principles outlined in your vision. Be transparent, accountable, and resilient when faced with challenges. Show dedication, perseverance, and a willingness to learn and grow. By embodying the vision, you inspire others to follow suit.

Summary

Crafting your vision is a transformative journey that requires self-reflection, clarity, effective communication, adaptability, and leading by example. By embracing these elements and leveraging thought leadership principles, you can create a vision that inspires, motivates, and drives positive change in yourself, your organization, and the wider world. Start your journey today and unlock your potential as a thought leader.

Chapter 2

Identifying Your Expertise

Introduction

Thought leadership is a powerful concept that revolves around sharing valuable insights, innovative ideas, and expertise in a particular field. To become a thought leader, one must first identify their expertise, which serves as the foundation for building credibility and influence. In this chapter, we will explore the key steps to identify your expertise and unleash your thought leadership potential.

1. Self-Reflection

Understanding Your Passions and Strengths: To identify your expertise, start by reflecting on your passions and strengths. Consider the topics or industries that genuinely interest you and where you excel. Think about the skills you have developed over the years and the knowledge you have acquired. By focusing on these areas, you can better understand your unique value proposition and the expertise you can offer.

2. Research and Stay Updated

Thought leaders are known for their deep knowledge and understanding of their chosen field. To identify your expertise, conduct thorough research and stay updated with the latest trends, developments, and emerging technologies within your industry. Engage in continuous learning through books, articles, podcasts, webinars, and attending relevant conferences or workshops. This ongoing knowledge acquisition will help you refine your expertise and stay ahead in your field.

3. Identify Your Unique Perspective

While it's important to stay informed about the latest industry trends, your thought leadership should also reflect your unique perspective. Identify what sets you apart from others in your field. What insights or experiences do you bring that others might not have? Embrace your individuality and use it to shape your expertise. By offering a fresh and distinct viewpoint, you can attract attention and establish yourself as a thought leader.

4. Share Your Knowledge

Content Creation and Thoughtful Engagement: Once you have identified your expertise, it's time to start sharing your knowledge with others. Thought leaders often use various media to disseminate their insights, such as writing articles, creating videos, hosting webinars, or speaking at conferences. Focus on creating valuable and informative content that resonates with your target audience. Engage in thoughtful discussions and networking opportunities to expand your reach and build relationships within your industry.

5. Embrace Continuous Growth and Learning

Thought leadership is not a destination but a continuous journey. To maintain your position as a thought leader, embrace a growth mindset and never stop learning. Stay open to new ideas, seek feedback from your audience, and adapt to the evolving needs of your industry. By constantly expanding your expertise and staying at the forefront of your field, you can continue to provide value and inspire others.

Summary

Identifying your expertise is a crucial step towards becoming a thought leader. By reflecting on your passions, conducting thorough research, embracing your unique perspective, and sharing your knowledge through various media, you can establish yourself as a trusted and influential voice within your industry. Remember, thought leadership is not just about personal success, but also about making a positive impact and contributing to the growth and development of your field. So, unleash your expertise, inspire others, and embark on an exciting journey towards thought leadership.

Demonstrating the Impact of Thought Leadership on Brand Credibility and Marketing Positioning

In today's fast-paced and highly competitive business landscape, establishing a strong brand credibility and effective marketing positioning is crucial for companies to stand out from the crowd. One effective strategy that has gained significant traction in recent years is thought leadership. By positioning themselves as industry experts and sharing valuable insights, companies can establish trust, credibility, and influence within their target market. In this chapter, we will delve into the impact of thought leadership on brand credibility and marketing positioning, exploring how this approach can elevate a company's reputation and drive business growth.

Understanding Thought Leadership

Thought leadership refers to the practice of sharing unique perspectives, innovative ideas, and expert knowledge that can positively impact an industry or community. It involves consistently creating and distributing high-quality content, such as articles, blog posts, whitepapers, or videos, that demonstrate a deep understanding of the industry's challenges, trends, and opportunities. By consistently providing valuable insights, thought leaders position themselves as trusted advisors and industry experts, garnering respect and credibility from their audience.

Building Brand Credibility

Thought leadership plays a pivotal role in building brand credibility. When a company's leaders consistently provide valuable and insightful content, they establish themselves as authoritative figures within their industry. This expertise helps to instill confidence in their target audience, demonstrating that they possess the knowledge and experience necessary to solve their customers' pain points. As a result, potential customers are more likely to trust and engage with a brand that showcases thought leadership, leading to increased brand credibility.

Enhancing Marketing Positioning

Thought leadership also has a significant impact on a company's marketing positioning. By consistently sharing valuable insights and perspectives, thought leaders position themselves as go-to resources for industry-related information. This positioning allows companies to differentiate themselves from competitors, as potential customers perceive them as more knowledgeable and trustworthy. Thought leadership content also enables companies to showcase their unique value proposition, highlighting their expertise and innovative solutions. This positioning can ultimately lead to increased brand awareness, customer loyalty, and a competitive advantage in the market.

Measuring the Impact

Demonstrating the impact of thought leadership on brand credibility and marketing positioning requires a comprehensive measurement strategy. Key performance indicators (KPIs) such as website traffic, social media engagement, lead generation, and customer feedback can provide valuable insights into the effectiveness of thought leadership initiatives. Analyzing these metrics allows companies to gauge the reach and impact of their thought leadership content, helping them refine their strategies and maximize their influence.

Summary

Thought leadership is a powerful tool for enhancing brand credibility and marketing positioning. By consistently sharing valuable insights and establishing themselves as industry experts, companies can build trust, credibility, and influence within their target market. Thought leadership not only helps differentiate a brand from competitors but also drives brand awareness, customer loyalty, and business growth. Therefore, investing in thought leadership initiatives should be an integral part of any company's marketing strategy.

Section 3
Setting Strategic Goals for Thought Leadership Journey

In today's digital age, establishing thought leadership has become crucial for individuals and organizations alike. Being recognized as a thought leader in your industry not only enhances your credibility but also opens up numerous opportunities for growth and influence. However, becoming a thought leader requires a well-defined strategy and clear goals. In this section, we will explore the process of setting strategic goals for your thought leadership journey, using the keywords "thought leadership" as our guiding principle.

1. Define Your Purpose

 The first step in setting strategic goals for thought leadership is to define your purpose. Ask yourself, why do you want to become a thought leader? What do you hope to achieve through your thought leadership journey? Understanding your purpose will help you align your goals accordingly and stay focused throughout the process.

2. Identify Your Target Audience

Thought leadership is all about providing valuable insights and expertise to a specific audience. To set effective goals, you need to identify your target audience. Who are the individuals or groups you want to influence and engage with? Knowing your audience will enable you to tailor your content and thought leadership efforts to their needs and preferences.

3. Research and Stay Informed

 To be a thought leader, you need to stay ahead of the curve in your industry. Set goals to regularly research and stay informed about the latest trends, developments, and challenges in your field. This will help you position yourself as a knowledgeable resource and enable you to provide valuable and timely insights to your audience.

4. Establish Your Unique Voice

Thought leadership requires you to have a unique perspective and voice. Set goals to develop and establish your own thought leadership style. Focus on what differentiates you from others in your industry and how you can deliver your expertise in a way that resonates with your audience. This will help you stand out and build a loyal following.

5. Create High-Quality Content

Content creation is at the heart of thought leadership. Set goals to consistently create high-quality content that showcases your expertise and provides value to your audience. This can include blog articles, whitepapers, videos, podcasts, or any other medium that aligns with your target audience's preferences. Aim for regularity and consistency in your content creation efforts.

6. Build a Strong Network

Thought leadership is not a solitary pursuit. Set goals to build and nurture a strong network of like-minded individuals, industry experts, and potential collaborators. Engage in networking events, conferences, and online communities to expand your reach and establish valuable connections. Collaborating with others can amplify your thought leadership efforts and open up new opportunities.

7. Measure and Adjust

Setting goals is not enough; you also need to measure your progress and adjust your strategies accordingly. Set goals to regularly review and analyze the impact of your thought leadership efforts. Monitor metrics such as website traffic, engagement levels, social media interactions, and feedback from your audience. Use this data to refine your approach and continuously improve your thought leadership journey.

Summary

Setting strategic goals for your thought leadership journey is essential for success. By defining your purpose, identifying your target audience, staying informed, establishing your unique voice, creating high-quality content, building a strong network, and measuring your progress, you can pave the way for becoming a recognized thought leader in your industry. Remember, thought leadership is a continuous journey, so set goals that are adaptable and aligned with your long-term aspirations.

Chapter 3

Defining Your Target Audience: A Thought Leadership Approach

Understanding and defining your target audience is crucial for the success of any venture. Thought leaders recognize the significance of this process and utilize it as a strategic tool to drive their business growth. In this chapter, we will explore the concept of defining your target audience from a thought leadership perspective, highlighting the importance of thorough research, effective communication, and staying ahead of the curve.

1. Understanding the Power of Thought Leadership

Thought leadership entails establishing oneself as an authority in a particular industry or domain. By positioning yourself as a thought leader, you gain credibility, influence, and the ability to shape conversations around your area of expertise. Defining your target audience is a fundamental step in this process, as it allows you to tailor your content and messaging to resonate with the right people.

2. Conducting In-Depth Research

To define your target audience effectively, conducting thorough research is essential. Dive deep into market analysis, consumer behavior, demographics, and psychographics. Understand the pain points, motivations, and aspirations of your potential customers. By gaining a comprehensive understanding of your target audience, you can create content that addresses their specific needs and desires.

3. Segmenting Your Audience

Segmentation is a critical aspect of defining your target audience. Instead of approaching your audience as a homogeneous group, divide them into distinct segments based on characteristics such as age, gender, location, interests, and buying behavior. This segmentation allows you to create tailored marketing campaigns that resonate with each segment, increasing the likelihood of engagement and conversion.

4. Effective Communication Strategies

Once you have identified your target audience segments, it's crucial to develop effective communication strategies to reach them. Thought leaders leverage various channels such as blogs, social media platforms, podcasts, and webinars to share their expertise and engage with their audience. Craft compelling content that addresses their pain points, offers valuable insights, and positions you as a trusted source of information.

5. Staying Ahead of the Curve

Thought leaders understand the importance of staying ahead of the curve when defining their target audience. Markets evolve, consumer preferences change, and new trends emerge. Continuously monitor the industry landscape, keep an eye on competitors, and adapt your strategies accordingly. By staying up-to-date and anticipating shifts in your target audience's preferences, you can maintain your thought leadership position and ensure your content remains relevant and impactful.

Summary

Defining your target audience is a crucial aspect of thought leadership. By conducting comprehensive research, segmenting your audience, and developing effective communication strategies, you can position yourself as an authority in your industry. Moreover, staying ahead of the curve allows you to adapt to changing market dynamics and maintain your thought leadership status. Embrace this strategic approach and unlock the potential for business growth and influence in your domain.

Building a Personal Brand That Aligns with Your Goals: A Journey towards Thought Leadership

In today's competitive world, it is becoming increasingly important to establish a strong personal brand that aligns with your goals. Your Personal brand is essentially your reputation, the way you present yourself to the world and the values and expertise you bring to the table. To truly stand out and become a thought leader in your industry, it is crucial to strategically build a personal brand that reflects your goals and aspirations.

Thought leadership has become a buzzword in recent years, and for good reason. Thought leaders are individuals who are recognized as experts in their field, and their opinions and insights hold weight and influence. Building a personal brand that aligns with thought leadership involves positioning yourself as an authority, someone who others look up to for guidance and expertise.

Here are some key steps to consider when building a personal brand that aligns with your goals and positions you as a thought leader:

1. Define Your Goals

Start by clearly defining your goals and what you want to achieve. Whether it's becoming a sought-after speaker, publishing a book, or being recognized as a go-to expert in your industry, having a clear vision of your goals will guide your personal branding efforts.

2. Identify Your Niche

In order to establish yourself as a thought leader, it is important to identify your niche. What specific area or expertise do you want to be known for? By narrowing down your focus, you can position yourself as an authority in that particular area, making it easier for others to associate you with that expertise.

3. Develop Your Unique Voice

Thought leaders have a distinct voice and perspective that sets them apart from others. It is essential to develop your own unique voice and communicate your ideas and insights in a way that resonates with your target audience. This will help you stand out and build credibility as a thought leader.

4. Share Valuable Content

Creating and sharing valuable content is a key component of building a personal brand aligned with thought leadership. Whether it's through blog posts, articles, podcasts, or videos, consistently sharing insightful and relevant content will establish you as an expert in your field and attract a loyal following.

5. Engage with Your Audience

Building a personal brand is not just about broadcasting your expertise; it's about engaging with your audience and building meaningful connections. Respond to comments, participate in discussions, and actively seek out opportunities to connect with others in your industry. This will help you build a community around your personal brand and strengthen your thought leadership position.

6. Network and Collaborate

Thought leaders often collaborate with others in their field to expand their reach and influence. Identify opportunities to collaborate with like-minded individuals or organizations, whether it's through partnerships, guest blogging, or speaking engagements. By associating yourself with other thought leaders, you can further enhance your personal brand and establish yourself as a trusted authority.

Summary

Building a personal brand that aligns with your goals and positions you as a thought leader requires time, effort, and consistency. It is a journey that involves continuously honing your expertise, sharing valuable insights, and engaging with your audience. By following these steps and staying true to your goals, you can build a personal brand that not only reflects your aspirations but also positions you as a thought leader in your industry.

Establishing Credibility and Trust: The Key to Thought Leadership

In today's digital age, where information is readily available at our fingertips, establishing credibility and trust has become more important than ever. As thought leaders, it is crucial to not only possess expertise in our respective fields but also to build a reputation as reliable sources of information. In this chapter, we will explore the significance of establishing credibility and trust and how it contributes to thought leadership.

1. Building Expertise

Thought leadership begins with building expertise in a particular field. By consistently expanding our knowledge, staying updated with the latest trends, and conducting thorough research, we can position ourselves as knowledgeable authorities. Demonstrating expertise through insightful content, such as whitepapers, research studies, and case studies, helps establish credibility and trust among our target audience.

2. Authenticity and Transparency

Authenticity and transparency play a vital role in establishing credibility and trust. Being genuine and open in our interactions with others fosters a sense of connection and reliability. Sharing personal experiences, successes, and failures can humanize our thought leadership, making it more relatable to our audience. By showcasing our true selves, we build trust and credibility that goes beyond mere expertise.

3. Consistent and Quality Content

Consistency and quality are essential elements in thought leadership. Regularly publishing high-quality content that is relevant, insightful, and valuable to our audience establishes us as a trusted source of information. Thought leaders should aim to provide innovative perspectives, industry insights, and practical solutions that address the needs and challenges of their target audience. By consistently delivering valuable content, we can reinforce our credibility and trustworthiness.

4. Engaging with the Community

Engaging with our community is crucial for establishing credibility and trust as thought leaders. Actively participating in industry events, conferences, and webinars allows us to share our knowledge, network with other professionals, and build relationships. Additionally, responding to comments, questions, and concerns on social media platforms and blog posts demonstrates our commitment to engaging with our audience, fostering trust, and building credibility.

5. Collaborations and Endorsements

Collaborating with other respected thought leaders in our field can significantly enhance our credibility. By aligning ourselves with established experts and seeking endorsements from credible sources, we can leverage their reputation to bolster our own. Participating in panel discussions, interviews, and podcasts with industry leaders not only expands our reach but also validates our expertise and solidifies trust among our audience.

Summary

Establishing credibility and trust is a fundamental aspect of thought leadership. By building expertise, being authentic and transparent, consistently delivering high-quality content, engaging with the community, and seeking collaborations and endorsements, we can solidify our position as trusted thought leaders. Thought leadership is not just about being knowledgeable; it is about being a reliable source of information, inspiring others, and making a positive impact in our respective fields.

Communicating Your Value Proposition through Thought Leadership

It is crucial to effectively communicate your value proposition to establish a strong foothold in the market. One effective way to achieve this is by leveraging thought leadership. By positioning yourself as a thought leader in your industry, you can not only showcase your expertise but also communicate your unique value proposition to your target audience. In this chapter, we will explore how thought leadership can be utilized to effectively communicate your value proposition.

1. Understanding Thought Leadership

To communicate your value proposition through thought leadership, it is essential to first understand what thought leadership entails. Thought leadership refers to the practice of sharing valuable insights, knowledge, and expertise to establish yourself as an authority and influencer in your field. It involves consistently delivering valuable content, ideas, and perspectives that resonate with your target audience.

2. Identifying Your Unique Value Proposition

Before you can effectively communicate your value proposition, it is crucial to identify and articulate what sets your offering apart from competitors. Your unique value proposition should clearly define the benefits and value that your product or service brings to customers. By understanding your value proposition, you can align your thought leadership content to emphasize these unique aspects.

3. Creating Engaging Thought Leadership Content

Thought leadership content serves as a powerful tool to communicate your value proposition. It allows you to showcase your expertise, provide valuable insights, and establish credibility among your audience. Create content such as blog posts, articles, whitepapers, videos, and podcasts that address industry challenges, offer practical solutions, and demonstrate your unique perspective. By consistently delivering high-quality content, you can effectively communicate your value proposition to your target audience.

4. Leveraging Multiple Channels

To maximize the impact of your thought leadership content, it is important to leverage multiple channels to reach your target audience. Utilize social media platforms, industry forums, webinars, and conferences to distribute and promote your content. Engage with your audience by participating in relevant discussions and addressing their queries. By utilizing various channels, you can expand your reach and effectively communicate your value proposition to a wider audience.

5. Building Relationships and Trust

Building relationships and establishing trust are key components of effective thought leadership. Engage with your audience by responding to comments, questions, and feedback. Encourage discussions and foster a sense of community around your thought leadership content. By actively participating in conversations, you can build trust, credibility, and loyalty among your audience, thus enhancing the communication of your value proposition.

Summary

Communicating your value proposition is essential for business success, and thought leadership offers a powerful approach to achieve this goal. By leveraging thought leadership, you can effectively showcase your expertise, establish credibility, and communicate your unique value proposition to your target audience. Through the creation of engaging thought leadership content and the utilization of various distribution channels, you can build relationships, foster trust, and ultimately drive business growth. Embrace thought leadership as a strategic tool in your communication efforts and unlock the potential to stand out in a crowded marketplace.

Section 4

Building Thought Leadership Content Marketing Strategy

Digital age has made information readily available at our fingertips, making thought leadership crucial for businesses and individuals alike. It not only helps you gain credibility and trust but also positions you as an authority in your industry. And what better way to showcase your expertise than through a well-crafted thought leadership content marketing strategy? In this section, we will delve into the key aspects of building thought leadership content marketing strategy.

1. Defining Thought Leadership

Before we dive into the strategy, let's first understand what thought leadership means. Thought leadership is the process of becoming a trusted authority in your field by consistently sharing valuable insights, knowledge, and expertise with your target audience. It goes beyond self-promotion and focuses on providing valuable content that educates, inspires, and influences others.

2. Identifying Your Niche

It is essential to identify your niche or area of expertise in the quest of building thought leadership content marketing strategy. What unique insights or perspectives can you bring to the table? By narrowing down your focus, you can target a specific audience and provide them with tailored content that addresses their pain points and challenges.

3. Creating Compelling Content

Content is at the core of any thought leadership strategy. It is crucial to create high-quality, informative, and engaging content that showcases your expertise. This can include blog posts, articles, whitepapers, case studies, videos, and podcasts. Remember to prioritize quality over quantity and maintain consistency in your content creation.

4. Leveraging Multiple Channels

While creating compelling content is essential, it is equally important to distribute it through various channels. Utilize social media platforms, industry forums, guest blogging, and email newsletters to reach a wider audience. Engage with your audience by participating in discussions, responding to comments, and sharing your content across relevant communities.

5. Collaborating and Networking

Building thought leadership is not a solitary endeavor. Collaborating with other industry experts, influencers, and thought leaders can significantly enhance your credibility. Look for opportunities to contribute to industry publications, participate in panel discussions, or host webinars. Networking with like-minded professionals can open doors to new partnerships and expand your reach.

6. Measuring and Analyzing Results

To ensure the effectiveness of your thought leadership content marketing strategy, it is crucial to measure and analyze your results. Monitor key metrics such as website traffic, engagement levels, social media reach, and lead generation. Adjust your strategy based on the insights gained and continuously refine your content to meet the evolving needs of your audience.

Summary

Building thought leadership through a well-executed content marketing strategy can establish you as a trusted authority in your industry. By consistently providing valuable insights and engaging with your target audience, you can cultivate a loyal following and drive business growth. Remember, thought leadership is an ongoing process that requires dedication, expertise, and a genuine commitment to adding value to your audience's lives.

Chapter 4

Developing a Consistent Voice and Message

Developing a consistent voice and message is crucial for individuals and businesses looking to establish themselves as thought leaders in their respective fields. Thought leadership offers a unique opportunity to showcase expertise, build credibility, and influence others within a specific industry or niche. In this chapter, we will delve into the importance of developing a consistent voice and message and how it can contribute to thought leadership.

1. Defining Thought Leadership

Before we dive into the significance of a consistent voice and message, it is essential to understand what thought leadership entails. Thought leadership refers to the ability to provide innovative ideas, insights, and perspectives that challenge the status quo. It goes beyond simply sharing knowledge; it involves offering a fresh and unique point of view that inspires others and establishes credibility.

2. Why Consistency Matters

Consistency is the key to building trust and credibility. When your audience sees a consistent voice and message across your content, they develop a sense of familiarity and reliability. Consistency helps position you as an authority figure and enables your audience to recognize and connect with your brand. By consistently delivering valuable and insightful content, you establish yourself as a trusted source of information, further enhancing your thought leadership position.

3. Crafting Your Voice

Developing a consistent voice is about finding your unique style and tone that resonates with your target audience. Your voice should reflect your expertise, values, and personality. It should be authentic, engaging, and distinct. Whether you choose a conversational or formal tone, your voice should remain consistent across various platforms, such as blog posts, social media, videos, and podcasts. This consistency will help your audience recognize and associate your content with your thought leadership brand.

4. Aligning Your Message

While your voice represents the style and tone of your content, your message is the core idea or concept you want to convey. Your message should be clear, concise, and aligned with your thought leadership goals. It should address the pain points and challenges faced by your audience, offering them valuable insights and solutions. By consistently aligning your message with your thought leadership objectives, you reinforce your authority and position yourself as a go-to resource in your industry.

5. Adapting to Different Channels

Consistency doesn't mean delivering the same content across all platforms. It means adapting your voice and message to suit the unique characteristics and requirements of each channel. For instance, your blog posts may be more detailed and in-depth, while your social media posts may be concise and engaging. By maintaining a consistent underlying message while tailoring the content to different platforms, you can effectively reach and engage with a wider audience.

Summary

Developing a consistent voice and message is crucial for establishing thought leadership. Consistency builds trust, credibility, and recognition among your audience. By crafting your unique voice, aligning your message with your thought leadership goals, and adapting to different channels, you can effectively position yourself as a thought leader in your industry, gaining influence and making a lasting impact.

Choosing the Right Platforms and Channels

By sharing valuable insights, expertise, and unique perspectives, thought leaders can build credibility and gain a loyal following. However, with numerous platforms and channels available, it can be overwhelming to determine the most effective ones to showcase your thought leadership. In this chapter, we will explore the key considerations when choosing the right platforms and channels to amplify your thought leadership.

1. Understand Your Target Audience

Before selecting platforms and channels, it is crucial to understand your target audience. Consider their demographics, preferences, and online behavior. Are they active on social media platforms like LinkedIn or Twitter? Do they prefer consuming long-form content through blogs or short videos on YouTube? By identifying where your audience spends their time, you can tailor your thought leadership content for maximum impact.

2. Leverage Social Media Platforms

Social media platforms play a significant role in thought leadership. LinkedIn, Twitter, and Facebook are popular choices for professionals, while Instagram and TikTok cater to a younger demographic. Each platform has its own strengths and limitations, so it's essential to choose the ones that align with your content strategy and audience. LinkedIn, for example, is ideal for sharing industry insights and engaging in professional discussions, while Instagram is more visual and can be used to showcase your expertise through captivating visuals and stories.

3. Consider Blogging and Guest Posting

Maintaining a blog on your website or contributing as a guest author on reputable platforms can greatly enhance your thought leadership efforts. Blogging allows you to dive deeper into topics and establish yourself as an authority in your niche. Guest posting on relevant industry websites can expose your expertise to a wider audience and help you connect with fellow thought leaders. Remember to optimize your blog content with relevant keywords to improve visibility and search engine rankings.

4. Explore Podcasting and Webinars:

Podcasting and webinars have gained immense popularity in recent years, offering thought leaders a unique opportunity to engage with their audience. Podcasts allow you to share your insights in an audio format, giving listeners the freedom to consume content on-the-go. Webinars, on the other hand, enable you to host live or pre-recorded video sessions, interact with attendees, and delve deeper into complex topics. These platforms and channels provide an interactive and personal touch, fostering a stronger connection with your audience.

5. Monitor and Evaluate

Lastly, it is essential to monitor and evaluate the performance of your chosen platforms and Channels. Utilize analytics tools to track engagement metrics, such as views, likes, comments, shares, and conversions. These data will help you identify which platforms are resonating with your audience and driving the most significant impact. Regularly reassess your strategy, experiment with new platforms, and adapt to evolving trends to ensure your thought leadership efforts remain effective.

Summary

Choosing the right platforms and channels is crucial for successful thought leadership. By understanding your target audience, leveraging social media platforms, blogging, exploring podcasts and webinars, and monitoring performance, you can effectively amplify your thought leadership and establish yourself as a reputable authority in your field. Remember, consistency, quality content, and adaptability are key to standing out in the ever-evolving digital landscape.

Creating Compelling Content: Blogs, Articles, and White Papers

Thought leadership not only enhances credibility but also helps to build a loyal audience. One effective way to achieve this is through creating compelling content, specifically through blogs, articles, and white papers. Let's delve into each of these media and explore how they can be utilized to showcase thought leadership.

Blogs

Blogs have emerged as a popular platform for sharing insights, knowledge, and expertise. They offer a more informal and conversational tone, allowing thought leaders to connect with their audience on a personal level. When crafting blog content, it is crucial to focus on providing value to readers. This can be achieved by addressing industry trends, sharing best practices, and offering practical tips. By consistently delivering high-quality content, thought leaders can establish themselves as go-to sources of information, building trust and credibility among their readership.

Articles

Articles are typically more formal and in-depth than blogs. They provide an opportunity to delve into complex topics and showcase expertise. When writing articles, it is important to conduct thorough research and present unique insights or perspectives. Thought leaders should aim to contribute new knowledge or challenge existing ideas within their field. By doing so, they can position themselves as forward-thinkers and industry influencers. Publishing articles in reputable industry publications or journals further enhances the thought leader's reputation and reach.

White Papers

White papers are comprehensive reports that delve into a specific topic, often addressing complex issues or offering solutions to industry challenges. These documents are highly regarded within professional circles and are an excellent tool for establishing thought leadership. Thought leaders can leverage white papers to showcase their expertise, provide in-depth analysis, and propose innovative ideas or strategies. By presenting well-researched and credible information, thought leaders can position themselves as authoritative voices within their industry.

Summary

Creating compelling content through blogs, articles, and white papers is an effective way to establish thought leadership. By consistently delivering valuable insights, thought leaders can build credibility, trust, and a loyal audience. It is important to focus on providing unique perspectives, challenging existing ideas, and offering practical solutions. By doing so, thought leaders can position themselves as industry influencers and be recognized as go-to sources of information within their respective fields.

Harnessing the Power of Social Media

In today's digital age, social media has become an integral part of our lives. From connecting with friends and family to staying updated with the latest news and trends, social media platforms have transformed the way we communicate and share information. However, social media is more than just a tool for personal use. It has the power to shape narratives, influence opinions, and drive businesses towards success. In this chapter, we will explore how thought leadership can be harnessed through social media to create meaningful impact and establish a strong online presence.

1. Understanding Thought Leadership in the Digital Era

Thought leadership is about becoming a trusted authority in your field, someone whose opinions and ideas are valued and respected. In the digital era, social media provides an unprecedented opportunity to establish thought leadership. By consistently sharing valuable insights, unique perspectives, and industry knowledge, individuals and businesses can position themselves as industry leaders and influencers within their respective niches.

2. Building a Thought Leadership Strategy on Social Media

To harness the power of social media for thought leadership, a strategic approach is essential. Here are some key steps to consider:

a) Identifying Your Niche: Determine your area of expertise and the specific industry or topic you want to focus on. This will help you carve out a niche where you can establish thought leadership.

b) Creating Engaging Content: Develop high-quality content that adds value to your audience. This can be in the form of blog articles, videos, podcasts, or infographics. By consistently sharing insightful content, you can attract a loyal following and establish yourself as a thought leader.

c) Leveraging Different Social Media Platforms: Each social media platform offers unique features and audiences. Tailor your content to suit the platform and engage with your audience effectively. Whether it's LinkedIn for professional networking or Instagram for visual storytelling, leverage the strengths of each platform to amplify your thought leadership.

d) Engaging in Conversations: Thought leadership is not a one-way street. Engage in conversations with your audience, respond to comments, and participate in relevant discussions. This will not only enhance your credibility but also help you understand your audience better.

e) Collaborating with Influencers: Collaborating with other thought leaders or influencers in your industry can amplify your reach and establish your authority. By partnering on projects, guest blogging, or participating in joint webinars, you can tap into their audience and expand your thought leadership.

3. Measuring Success and Adapting Strategies

To ensure your thought leadership efforts on social media are effective, it's crucial to measure key metrics and adapt your strategies accordingly. Monitor engagement rates, follower growth, website traffic, and conversions to gauge the impact of your content. Use analytics tools provided by social media platforms to gain insights into your audience's preferences and tailor your content accordingly.

Summary

Harnessing the power of social media for thought leadership can be a game-changer for individuals and businesses seeking to establish themselves as industry leaders. By following a strategic approach, creating engaging content, leveraging different social media platforms, engaging in conversations, and collaborating with influencers, you can build a strong online presence and make a meaningful impact in your field. So, embrace the power of social media, position yourself as a thought leader, and unlock new opportunities for success.

Leverage Podcasts, Webinars and Videos

Leveraging various multimedia platforms is crucial for establishing thought leadership in any industry. Podcasts, webinars, and videos have become powerful tools for disseminating knowledge, sharing insights, and building credibility. By harnessing these platforms effectively, individuals and businesses can establish themselves as thought leaders, gaining a competitive edge and attracting a loyal following. Let's explore how podcasts, webinars, and videos can be leveraged to enhance thought leadership.

Podcasts have gained immense popularity in recent years, offering a convenient way for thought leaders to share their expertise. With the rise of platforms like Spotify, Apple Podcasts, and Google Podcasts, podcasts have become easily accessible to a vast audience. As a thought leader, hosting your own podcast allows you to share your unique perspectives, industry insights, and experiences with a global audience. By consistently delivering valuable content, you can position yourself as an authority in your field and build a loyal community of listeners.

Webinars, on the other hand, provide an interactive platform for thought leaders to engage directly with their audience. These live or pre-recorded online seminars enable participants to learn from experts, ask questions, and gain valuable insights. As a thought leader, hosting webinars allows you to showcase your knowledge, establish credibility, and establish yourself as a go-to resource in your industry. By providing valuable and actionable information, you can foster a sense of trust with your audience, solidifying your position as a thought leader.

Videos, whether in the form of recorded presentations, interviews, or educational content, have become increasingly popular in thought leadership strategies. With platforms like YouTube and social media channels, videos offer an engaging way to connect with your audience visually and audibly. By creating high-quality videos that provide valuable insights and actionable advice, you can captivate your audience and establish yourself as a trusted expert. Videos also allow you to showcase your personality, passion, and expertise, creating a deeper connection with your viewers.

When leveraging podcasts, webinars, and videos for thought leadership, it's essential to focus on delivering valuable content consistently. Thought leaders must strive to provide unique insights, actionable tips, and solutions to their audience's pain points. By addressing current industry trends, challenges, and opportunities, you can position yourself as a forward-thinking expert, gaining the trust and respect of your audience.

Additionally, actively engaging with your audience through these platforms is crucial for building a strong thought leadership presence. Encourage listeners, viewers, and participants to share their feedback, questions, and suggestions. Responding to comments, hosting Q&A sessions, and participating in discussions further establishes your expertise and fosters a sense of community.

Summary

Leveraging podcasts, webinars, and videos is an effective way to establish thought leadership in today's digital landscape. By consistently delivering valuable content, engaging with your audience, and showcasing your expertise, you can position yourself as a trusted authority in your industry. Embrace these multimedia platforms, harness their power, and watch your thought leadership grow.

Section 5

Establishing Authority and Credibility

In our today's highly competitive business landscape, establishing authority and credibility is crucial for individuals and organizations to stand out from the crowd. One powerful strategy that has gained significant traction in recent years is thought leadership. By becoming a thought leader in your industry, you can position yourself as an expert and trusted source of information, ultimately enhancing your authority and credibility. Let's delve into the world of thought leadership and explore how it can empower you to establish a strong presence in your field.

What is Thought Leadership?

Be reminded once again that, Thought leadership is a concept that goes beyond merely sharing knowledge or expertise. It involves shaping and influencing industry conversations, driving innovation, and providing valuable insights that inspire others. Thought leaders are individuals or organizations that consistently deliver unique perspectives, original ideas, and forward-thinking solutions. By consistently offering valuable insights, thought leaders become go-to sources for industry-related information, earning the trust and respect of their peers and target audiences.

The Power of Thought Leadership

Thought leadership is not just about gaining recognition; it is about establishing authority and credibility. When you position yourself as a thought leader, you take on the responsibility of shaping industry trends and influencing the decision-making process. This influence allows you to gain a competitive edge, attract new opportunities, and build a strong network of like-minded professionals. Thought leadership also enables you to establish your personal or organizational brand as a trusted resource, creating a loyal following and enhancing your credibility in the eyes of your audience.

Here are Key Strategies for Establishing Authority and Credibility through Thought Leadership:

1. Identify Your Niche: To establish authority, it is essential to identify your niche and focus on a specific area within your industry. By narrowing your expertise, you can become a go-to resource for that particular subject, positioning yourself as an authority figure.

2. Create High-Quality Content: Thought leaders consistently produce high-quality content that offers valuable insights and solutions. This can include blog posts, articles, whitepapers, videos, podcasts, or even social media content. By sharing your expertise through various channels, you can reach a wider audience and solidify your position as a thought leader.

3. Engage and Collaborate: Building a strong network of professionals within your industry is crucial for establishing authority. Engage in conversations, attend industry events, and collaborate with other thought leaders to foster relationships and increase your visibility.

4. Stay Ahead of the Curve: Thought leaders are known for their ability to anticipate industry trends and provide innovative solutions. Continuously educate yourself, stay updated on the latest developments, and share your forward-thinking ideas to maintain your credibility as an authority in your field.

5. Be Authentic and Transparent: Thought leadership is built on trust. Be authentic in your communication, share your experiences (both successes and failures), and be transparent about your perspectives. This honesty will resonate with your audience and further establish your credibility.

Summary

Establishing authority and credibility through thought leadership is a powerful strategy that can help you stand out in today's competitive landscape. By consistently sharing valuable insights, engaging with your industry, and staying ahead of the curve, you can position yourself as an expert and trusted resource. Embrace the power of thought leadership and unlock new opportunities to establish your authority and credibility in your field.

Chapter 5

Collaborating with Industry Influencers and Experts

In the present highly competitive business landscape, staying relevant and influential is crucial for any industry. One effective way to achieve this is by collaborating with industry influencers and experts, who possess the knowledge, experience, and authoritative voice that can propel your brand to new heights. This strategic partnership not only enhances your credibility but also enables you to tap into their vast network of followers, amplifying your reach and impact. Welcome to the world of thought leadership, where collaboration with industry influencers and experts can be a game-changer for your business.

Thought leadership, a term widely used in the business world, refers to individuals or organizations who are recognized as experts in their respective fields. These thought leaders possess deep insights, innovative ideas, and a unique perspective that sets them apart from the rest. Collaborating with them not only allows you to tap into their wealth of knowledge but also positions your brand as a trusted authority within your industry.

The benefits of collaborating with industry influencers and experts for thought leadership are manifold. Firstly, it provides an opportunity to leverage their expertise and credibility to enhance your brand's reputation. When you align yourself with recognized thought leaders, their endorsement of your brand or product carries immense weight, instilling trust and confidence in your target audience.

Secondly, collaborating with industry influencers and experts can significantly expand your reach. These thought leaders have a loyal following and a vast network of connections that can help you tap into new markets and demographics. By associating with them, you gain access to their audience, allowing you to extend your brand's visibility and influence beyond your existing customer base.

Furthermore, collaborating with thought leaders can spark innovation within your organization. By engaging in meaningful conversations and exchanging ideas, you gain valuable insights that can inspire new strategies, products, or services. This collaboration fosters a culture of continuous learning and growth, enabling you to stay ahead of the competition and drive innovation within your industry.

To effectively collaborate with industry influencers and experts, it is crucial to approach them with a genuine intent to build a mutually beneficial relationship. Thought leaders are often inundated with requests, so it's essential to demonstrate the value you bring to the table. Show them how your collaboration can benefit both parties and contribute to the industry as a whole. Be prepared to provide tangible examples of how your brand aligns with their values and goals.

Summary

Collaborating with industry influencers and experts is a powerful strategy to unlock the potential of thought leadership. By leveraging their expertise, credibility, and network, you can enhance your brand's reputation, expand your reach, and drive innovation within your industry. Thought leaders possess the ability to inspire, influence, and shape the future of their respective fields. So, don't hesitate to reach out, collaborate, and embark on a journey towards thought leadership that will propel your business to new heights.

Speaking Engagement and Thought Leadership Events

In highly competitive business landscape, establishing oneself as a thought leader has become increasingly crucial. Thought leadership is all about being recognized as an authority in a specific field, possessing deep knowledge and expertise, and consistently sharing valuable insights with others. One of the most effective ways to showcase thought leadership is through speaking engagements and thought leadership events.

Speaking engagements provide thought leaders with a platform to share their expertise, ideas, and perspectives with a wider audience. These events allow thought leaders to engage with industry professionals, peers, and potential clients, fostering meaningful connections and establishing themselves as trusted sources of information. By delivering compelling presentations, thought leaders can inspire and educate others, leaving a lasting impact on the audience.

Thought leadership events, on the other hand, are specifically designed to bring together thought leaders from various industries or disciplines. These events provide a unique opportunity for networking, collaboration, and knowledge exchange. Attending such events allows thought leaders to stay up-to-date with the latest trends, gain insights from other experts, and broaden their perspectives.

When it comes to speaking engagements and thought leadership events, there are several key considerations to keep in mind. First and foremost, it is essential to identify the right target audience. Understanding who would benefit the most from your expertise ensures that your message resonates with the right people. Moreover, selecting the right platforms and events that align with your niche and industry is crucial for positioning yourself as a thought leader.

Preparing for a speaking engagement or thought leadership event requires careful planning and preparation. Thought leaders should invest time in crafting compelling presentations that showcase their unique insights and expertise. It is essential to deliver a clear and concise message that captures the audience's attention and provides actionable takeaways. A well-prepared presentation not only establishes credibility but also helps to establish a strong personal brand.

In addition to speaking engagements and thought leadership events, leveraging digital platforms is equally important. Creating valuable content on various media such as blogs, podcasts, and videos helps thought leaders reach a wider audience and establish their authority in the digital realm. Sharing thought-provoking ideas, industry insights, and practical tips through these channels further solidifies their position as thought leaders.

Lastly, it is crucial for thought leaders to continuously refine their knowledge and expertise. Staying updated with the latest industry trends, conducting research, and engaging in continuous learning are essential for maintaining thought leadership status. By consistently expanding their knowledge base and challenging conventional wisdom, thought leaders can continue to provide valuable insights and remain at the forefront of their respective fields.

Summary

Speaking engagements and thought leadership events offer powerful platforms for thought leaders to share their expertise, connect with industry professionals, and establish themselves as authorities in their fields. By carefully selecting the right platforms, preparing compelling presentations, and leveraging digital channels, thought leaders can effectively position themselves as valuable resources for industry insights and innovative ideas. Continuous learning and staying up-to-date with industry trends are vital for thought leaders to maintain their status and continue making a significant impact.

Publishing a Book or Authoring Reports

In the realm of thought leadership, one avenue that holds significant potential for establishing oneself as an expert in a particular field is publishing a book or authoring reports. Thought leaders are recognized for their innovative ideas, insights, and expertise, and leveraging the power of the written word can help amplify their influence and impact. In this chapter, we will explore the significance of publishing on the subject thought leadership, discuss the benefits it offers, and provide valuable insights for aspiring authors and thought leaders.

1. Establishing Credibility and Authority

Publishing a book or authoring reports is an effective way to establish credibility and authority within a specific domain. By sharing your expertise and knowledge through written content, you position yourself as a thought leader, gaining recognition and respect from peers, professionals, and the wider audience. A well-researched and thoughtfully crafted publication can serve as a tangible testament to your expertise, elevating your profile and opening doors to new opportunities.

2. Expanding Reach and Influence

Thought leaders strive to make an impact by influencing and inspiring others. Publishing offers a platform to reach a broader audience and extend your influence beyond traditional boundaries. Books and reports have the potential to reach a global readership, allowing you to share your unique ideas, insights, and perspectives with a wider range of individuals. This increased visibility can attract new followers, collaborators, and even potential clients, enhancing your thought leadership journey.

3. Cultivating Thought-Provoking Ideas

Writing a book or authoring reports compels thought leaders to dive deeper into their subject matter, fostering a process of exploration and discovery. The act of articulating your ideas in a coherent and structured manner challenges you to refine your thinking, explore new angles, and develop innovative concepts. This intellectual exercise not only enriches your own understanding but also enables you to contribute thought-provoking ideas to the broader discourse within your field.

4. Building a Personal Brand

Thought leadership encompasses not only expertise but also the cultivation of a strong personal brand. Publishing a book or reports can significantly contribute to building and strengthening your personal brand. Consistently sharing your ideas and insights through written content establishes you as a go-to resource within your industry or niche. As your reputation grows, your personal brand gains recognition, positioning you as a trusted authority and driving further opportunities for growth.

5. Generating Speaking and Collaboration Opportunities

Publishing a book or authoring reports can open doors to various speaking engagements, conferences, and collaborative projects. Thought leaders are often sought after as keynote speakers or panelists at industry events, where they can further showcase their expertise and engage with like-minded professionals. Additionally, publishing provides opportunities for collaboration with other thought leaders, leading to the creation of valuable networks and partnerships that can amplify your impact.

Summary

Publishing a book or authoring reports is a powerful tool for thought leaders to establish their credibility, expand their reach, cultivate ideas, build a personal brand, and generate speaking and collaboration opportunities. By leveraging the written word, thought leaders can contribute to the broader discourse within their field, inspire others, and leave a lasting impact. So, if you aspire to be a thought leader, consider embarking on the journey of publishing, and let your ideas shape the world.

Section 6

Networking Engagement

In today's interconnected world, networking has become an essential aspect of personal and professional growth. Whether you are an entrepreneur, a professional, or an aspiring thought leader, building meaningful connections and engaging with others in your field is crucial for success. In this section, we will explore the concept of networking engagement from a thought leadership perspective, highlighting the importance of thought leadership in fostering valuable connections and enhancing your networking efforts.

Thought leadership, as a term, refers to individuals who are recognized as experts in their respective fields. These thought leaders possess deep knowledge, insights, and innovative ideas that they share with others, positioning themselves as trusted authorities. By leveraging their expertise, thought leaders inspire and influence others, shaping the conversation and driving positive change within their industries.

When it comes to networking engagement, thought leadership plays a pivotal role. By positioning yourself as a thought leader, you can attract like-minded individuals, industry professionals, and potential collaborators who are interested in your ideas and insights. This not only expands your network but also creates opportunities for collaboration, partnerships, and even career advancements.

Here are a few key strategies to enhance your networking engagement through thought leadership:

1. Share Valuable Content

Thought leaders are known for consistently sharing valuable content that educates, inspires, and challenges existing norms. By creating and sharing thought-provoking articles, blog posts, videos, or podcasts, you can establish yourself as a reliable source of information and attract a diverse audience interested in engaging with your ideas.

2. Participate in Industry Events

Actively participating in industry events, conferences, and webinars allows you to showcase your expertise and engage with other professionals in your field. By speaking at these events or participating in panel discussions, you can demonstrate your thought leadership and connect with like-minded individuals who share similar interests.

3. Engage on Social Media

Social media platforms provide a powerful medium for networking engagement. As a thought leader, actively engage with your followers, respond to comments, and initiate conversations on relevant topics. By consistently sharing valuable insights and engaging with others, you can attract a loyal following and expand your network.

4. Collaborate with Peers

Networking is not just about building connections; it's also about nurturing them. Seek opportunities to collaborate with other thought leaders or industry professionals who complement your expertise. By working together on projects, sharing resources, and cross-promoting each other's work, you can leverage each other's networks and reach a wider audience.

5. Offer Mentorship and Guidance

Thought leaders are often seen as mentors and guides within their fields. By offering mentorship or guidance to aspiring professionals, you not only contribute to the growth of others but also establish yourself as a valuable resource and connector within your network.

Summary

Networking engagement and thought leadership go hand in hand. By positioning yourself as a thought leader and leveraging your expertise to share valuable insights, you can attract a network of like-minded individuals, industry professionals, and potential collaborators. Embrace the power of thought leadership in your networking efforts, and watch as your connections and opportunities multiply.

Chapter 6

Fostering Dialogue

In today's fast-paced and interconnected world, fostering dialogue has become more crucial than ever before. As thought leaders, it is our responsibility to initiate and nurture meaningful conversations that can drive positive change and innovation. By utilizing the power of dialogue, we can bridge gaps, understand diverse perspectives, and pave the way for collaborative solutions.

Thought leadership, a term gaining prominence in recent years, refers to individuals or organizations that are recognized as experts in their respective fields. These thought leaders possess a deep understanding of industry trends, challenges, and opportunities, and they actively engage in shaping the discourse surrounding these topics. By leveraging their expertise, they inspire others and drive conversations that have the potential to shape the future.

When it comes to fostering dialogue, thought leaders play a crucial role. They have the ability to spark conversations on critical issues, challenge existing norms, and encourage others to think outside the box. By sharing their insights and experiences, thought leaders can inspire others to join the conversation and contribute their unique perspectives.

One of the key aspects of fostering dialogue is creating a safe and inclusive environment where individuals feel comfortable expressing their thoughts and ideas. Thought leaders can set the tone by actively listening, respecting diverse viewpoints, and encouraging open-mindedness. By doing so, they create a space that encourages constructive discussions and enables the exchange of ideas without fear of judgment.

Another important aspect of fostering dialogue is the ability to ask thought-provoking questions. Thought leaders have a knack for identifying gaps in knowledge or understanding and posing questions that challenge the status quo. By asking the right questions, they stimulate critical thinking and encourage others to explore new possibilities. This can lead to breakthroughs, innovative solutions, and the emergence of new perspectives.

Thought leaders also have the power to facilitate dialogue by bringing together diverse stakeholders. By organizing conferences, seminars, or virtual events, they provide platforms for individuals from different backgrounds to come together and engage in meaningful conversations. These events foster networking opportunities, encourage collaboration, and create a fertile ground for generating new ideas.

Summary

Fostering dialogue is an essential aspect of thought leadership. Thought leaders have the ability to drive conversations, challenge existing norms, and inspire others to think differently. By creating inclusive environments, asking thought-provoking questions, and facilitating dialogue among diverse stakeholders, thought leaders can contribute to positive change and innovation. As we navigate the complexities of our world, let us embrace the power of dialogue and leverage our thought leadership to make a lasting impact.

Responding to Feedback and Criticism

As a thought leader in your industry, it is essential to not only share your expertise and insights but also to embrace feedback and criticism. Responding to feedback in a thoughtful and constructive manner not only showcases your thought leadership but also demonstrates your commitment to continuous improvement. In this chapter, we will explore the significance of responding to feedback and criticism in a way that enhances your thought leadership position.

1. The Importance of Feedback

Thought leaders understand that feedback is a valuable source of information. Whether positive or negative, feedback provides insights into how your ideas, products, or services are perceived by your audience. By actively seeking feedback and valuing it as a learning opportunity, you can enhance your thought leadership by continuously refining and improving your offerings.

2. Embracing Constructive Criticism

Thought leaders recognize that constructive criticism is an opportunity for growth. Rather than becoming defensive or dismissive, thought leaders listen attentively to critics and analyze their feedback objectively. By embracing constructive criticism, you can demonstrate your thought leadership by showing humility and a willingness to learn from others.

3. Responding with Empathy and Understanding

Thought leaders prioritize empathy and understanding when responding to feedback and criticism. By acknowledging the perspective of the critic and understanding their concerns, you can foster meaningful conversations and build credibility. Thought leaders are skilled at engaging in open dialogue, addressing concerns, and providing thoughtful responses that show respect for differing opinions.

4. Leveraging Feedback for Thought Leadership

Thought leaders understand that feedback can be a catalyst for innovation and thought-provoking discussions. By actively incorporating feedback into your thought leadership content, you can demonstrate your ability to adapt and respond to the needs of your audience. Thought leaders leverage feedback to generate new ideas, challenge existing paradigms, and provide valuable insights that resonate with their followers.

5. Transparency and Accountability

Thought leaders value transparency and accountability when responding to feedback and criticism. By openly acknowledging any mistakes or shortcomings, you can establish trust and credibility with your audience. Thought leaders take responsibility for their actions and use feedback as an opportunity to showcase their commitment to improvement and growth.

Summary

Responding to feedback and criticism is an integral part of thought leadership. By embracing feedback, embracing constructive criticism with empathy and understanding, and leveraging it to enhance your thought leadership content, you can establish yourself as a trusted and respected authority in your field. Remember, thought leaders actively seek feedback, learn from it, and consistently adapt to meet the evolving needs of their audience.

Building Communities

In new era of the interconnected world, building communities has become a crucial aspect of both personal and professional growth. As thought leaders, we have a unique opportunity to not only shape the discourse surrounding community building but also actively contribute to its development. In this chapter, we will explore the significance of building communities and how thought leadership can play a pivotal role in this process.

1. Understanding the Power of Communities

Communities have always existed, serving as a source of support, collaboration, and growth for individuals. However, in the digital age, the concept of community has taken on a whole new dimension. Online platforms and social media have made it easier than ever to connect with like-minded individuals, fostering the creation of virtual communities that transcend geographical boundaries. Thought leaders recognize the power of these communities to drive change, inspire innovation, and create a sense of belonging.

2. Thought Leadership in Community Building

Thought leadership goes beyond simply sharing knowledge; it involves actively influencing and shaping the conversations within a community. As thought leaders, we have a responsibility to provide valuable insights, challenge existing norms, and inspire others to take action. By leveraging our expertise and experiences, we can guide communities towards meaningful discussions, encourage collaboration, and foster an environment where diverse perspectives are welcomed and respected.

3. Nurturing Engagement and Collaboration

Building communities is not a one-way street; it requires active participation and engagement from all members. Thought leaders can act as catalysts for engagement, providing thought-provoking content, initiating conversations, and encouraging collaboration. By sharing our knowledge and experiences, we can inspire others to share their insights, leading to a collective growth of the community as a whole. Thought leaders have the ability to create a safe and inclusive space where individuals feel comfortable expressing their opinions, thereby fostering a vibrant and dynamic community.

4. Driving Change and Impact

Communities have the potential to drive significant change and impact. Thought leaders can leverage their influence to rally communities around a shared vision, inspire action, and create positive change. By providing guidance, thought leaders can empower community members to take ownership of their ideas, projects, and initiatives, resulting in a collective effort towards achieving common goals. With thought leadership at the helm, communities can become powerful agents of change, making a tangible difference in various domains.

Summary

Building communities is an integral part of thought leadership. By understanding the power of communities, nurturing engagement, and driving change, thought leaders can actively contribute to the development of vibrant and impactful communities. Through our expertise and influence, we can shape the conversations, inspire collaboration, and foster an environment where individuals thrive and grow together. Let us embrace our role as thought leaders and make a positive impact on the communities we are a part of.

Leveraging Partnership to Expand Your Reach and Influence

In the competitive business landscape, establishing a strong presence and expanding your reach and influence has become crucial for success. While implementing effective marketing strategies and utilizing various channels can certainly help, one powerful approach that shouldn't be overlooked is leveraging partnerships. By collaborating with other industry leaders and experts, you can tap into their networks, expertise, and credibility to amplify your own brand and influence. In this chapter, we will explore the concept of leveraging partnerships as a means to expand your reach and influence, with a focus on the thought leadership aspect.

Thought leadership has emerged as a key strategy for businesses aiming to establish themselves as industry authorities and gain a competitive edge. It involves positioning yourself or your organization as a trusted source of knowledge, insights, and innovative ideas within your field. By becoming a thought leader, you not only enhance your reputation but also attract a loyal following of customers, clients, and even potential partners.

When it comes to leveraging partnerships to enhance your thought leadership, there are several key steps to consider:

1.   Identify Relevant Partners

Look for individuals or organizations that complement your expertise and share similar values and goals. Seek out partners who have established themselves as thought leaders in their respective areas, as their credibility will reflect positively on your brand.

2. Establish Mutually Beneficial Relationships

Building strong partnerships requires a mutually beneficial approach. Determine what value you can bring to the table and how your collaboration can benefit both parties. This could involve sharing resources, co-creating content, or cross-promoting each other's work.

3. Collaborate on Content Creation:

One effective way to leverage partnerships is by collaborating on content creation. By combining your expertise and perspectives, you can produce high-quality, insightful content that resonates with your target audience. This could include co-authored articles, joint webinars, or podcasts.

4. Tap into Partner Networks

One of the greatest advantages of partnerships is the ability to tap into each other's networks. By sharing your partner's content, engaging with their audience, and participating in joint events, you can significantly expand your reach and influence. This cross-pollination of audiences can lead to new opportunities and increased visibility.

5. Engage in Speaking Opportunities

Another effective way to leverage partnerships is by participating in speaking engagements together. This could involve hosting joint webinars, speaking at industry conferences or events, or even organizing panel discussions. By sharing the stage with your partner, you enhance your credibility and reach a broader audience.

6. Maintain Consistent Communication

To ensure the success of your partnerships, it is crucial to maintain consistent communication. Regularly communicate with your partners to align strategies, discuss upcoming opportunities, and provide feedback. This will help foster a strong, collaborative relationship built on trust and shared goals.

Summary

Leveraging partnerships can be a game-changer when it comes to expanding your reach and influence as a thought leader. By collaborating with other industry experts, you can tap into their networks, knowledge, and credibility to enhance your own brand. Remember to identify relevant partners, establish mutually beneficial relationships, collaborate on content creation, tap into partner networks, engage in speaking opportunities, and maintain consistent communication. With the right partnerships in place, you can amplify your thought leadership efforts and make a lasting impact in your industry.

Section 7

Harnessing the Power of Thought Leadership for Client Acquisition

Thought leadership has become a buzzword in the business world, and for good reason. It is a powerful tool that can greatly benefit businesses, particularly in terms of client acquisition. In this section, we will explore the concept of thought leadership and how it can be harnessed to attract and acquire clients.

Thought leadership refers to the practice of positioning oneself or one's business as a trusted authority in a particular industry or field. It involves sharing valuable insights, knowledge, and expertise with the aim of influencing and guiding others. By establishing oneself as a thought leader, businesses can gain credibility, build trust, and ultimately attract new clients.

So, how can thought leadership be used to acquire clients? Let's delve into some key strategies:

1. Providing Valuable Content

Thought leaders are known for sharing valuable content that educates and solves problems for their target audience. By consistently offering high-quality content such as blog posts, articles, whitepapers, and videos, businesses can demonstrate their expertise and attract potential clients who are seeking solutions to their challenges.

2. Building Trust and Credibility

Thought leadership is all about establishing trust and credibility. By consistently delivering valuable insights and demonstrating industry knowledge, businesses can position themselves as trusted advisors. This trust can then translate into client acquisition, as potential clients are more likely to choose a thought leader they trust over competitors.

3. Networking and Collaboration

Engaging with other thought leaders in the industry can be mutually beneficial. By collaborating on projects, participating in industry events, and networking with like-minded individuals, businesses can expand their reach and attract clients who value the collective expertise of thought leaders.

4. Leveraging Social Media

Social media platforms provide an excellent opportunity to showcase thought leadership. By sharing content, engaging in discussions, and actively participating in relevant communities, businesses can increase their visibility, attract followers, and ultimately convert them into clients.

5. Speaking Engagements and Webinars

Thought leaders are often invited to speak at conferences, webinars, and industry events. These opportunities not only help to establish credibility but also provide a platform to showcase expertise and attract potential clients who are in attendance.

Harnessing the power of thought leadership for client acquisition requires consistency, dedication, and a genuine desire to provide value to the target audience. By positioning oneself as a trusted authority and consistently delivering valuable insights, businesses can attract and acquire clients who recognize the expertise and value they bring to the table.

Summary

Thought leadership is a powerful tool that can significantly impact client acquisition. By providing valuable content, building trust, networking, leveraging social media, and participating in speaking engagements, businesses can harness the power of thought leadership to attract and acquire clients. So, start sharing your knowledge, insights, and expertise to position yourself as a thought leader and watch your client acquisition efforts flourish.

Chapter 7

Understanding Your Audience

In the realm of thought leadership, understanding your audience is a crucial aspect that cannot be overlooked. Whether you are a business professional, a content creator, or a marketer, having a deep understanding of your target audience is paramount to effectively engaging and influencing them. In this chapter, we will explore the significance of understanding your audience from a thought leadership standpoint, and how it can elevate your strategies to new heights.

1. The Essence of Thought Leadership

Thought leadership entails being a trusted authority in your field, providing valuable insights and innovative ideas that shape and influence the industry. To achieve this, you must have a profound understanding of your audience's needs, challenges, and aspirations. By addressing their pain points and offering solutions, you establish yourself as a thought leader who genuinely cares about their success.

2. Identifying Your Target Audience

Before you can understand your audience, you must first identify who they are. Conduct thorough market research to gain insights into demographics, preferences, behavior patterns, and pain points. The data will help you create buyer personas or customer profiles that embody your ideal audience segments. By doing so, you can tailor your thought leadership content to resonate with their specific needs and interests.

3. Listening and Gathering Feedback

Thought leaders actively engage with their audience by listening and gathering feedback. This can be done through surveys, social media interactions, or even hosting webinars and events. By listening to your audience, you gain valuable insights into their opinions, challenges, and desires. This feedback loop allows you to refine your thought leadership approach and ensure that your content remains relevant and impactful.

4. Tailoring Your Content Strategy

Understanding your audience enables you to tailor your content strategy for maximum impact. By knowing their preferred communication channels, content formats, and topics of interest, you can create thought-provoking content that resonates deeply with them. Whether it's through blog posts, podcasts, videos, or social media campaigns, your thought leadership content should serve as a valuable resource that addresses their pain points and offers actionable insights.

5. Building Trust and Credibility

Thought leadership goes beyond simply sharing knowledge; it is about building trust and credibility with your audience. By understanding their needs and consistently delivering valuable content, you establish yourself as an authority figure they can rely on. This trust and credibility will not only foster loyalty but also encourage your audience to actively engage with your content, share it with others, and seek your guidance in their decision-making processes.

Summary

Understanding your audience is a fundamental aspect of thought leadership. By comprehending their needs, challenges, and aspirations, you can create impactful content that resonates deeply with them. This understanding allows you to build trust, credibility, and long-lasting relationships with your audience, ultimately positioning you as a thought leader in your industry. Embrace this knowledge and let it guide your thought leadership journey towards success.

Conducting Audience Research and Understanding Client Personas

Understanding your audience and client personas is crucial for any organization to thrive. Conducting thorough audience research not only helps in tailoring marketing strategies but also enables businesses to build meaningful connections with their target customers. In this chapter, we will delve into the significance of audience research and client personas from a thought leadership perspective, exploring how these practices can drive success and foster innovation.

Thought leaders, who are recognized as experts and visionaries in their respective fields, understand the importance of audience research as a foundation for their insights and ideas. By conducting thorough research on their target audience, thought leaders gain valuable insights into their preferences, needs, and pain points. This research enables them to develop a deep understanding of their audience's motivations, allowing them to craft content and strategies that resonate with their specific target group.

To conduct effective audience research, thought leaders employ various methodologies such as surveys, interviews, and data analysis. Surveys and interviews provide direct feedback from the audience, helping to identify their preferences, challenges, and aspirations. Additionally, analyzing data from social media platforms, website analytics, and industry reports can offer valuable insights into audience behaviors and trends.

Once the audience research is complete, thought leaders can create client personas – fictional representations of their ideal customers. These personas are built based on the data collected during the research, incorporating demographic information, psychographics, and behavioral patterns. Client personas enable thought leaders to humanize their audience, making it easier to empathize and connect with them on a deeper level.

Understanding client personas is a powerful tool for thought leaders to tailor their content, products, and services to meet their audience's specific needs. By segmenting their audience into different personas, thought leaders can personalize their messaging and offerings, ensuring that they resonate with each segment. This targeted approach not only enhances the overall customer experience but also increases engagement and conversions.

Moreover, client personas aid thought leaders in identifying new opportunities for innovation. By analyzing the pain points and challenges faced by their audience, thought leaders can uncover gaps in the market and develop innovative solutions. This proactive approach to problem-solving positions thought leaders as industry pioneers, driving the conversation forward and establishing their authority in their respective domains.

Summary

Conducting audience research and understanding client personas are essential practices for thought leaders aiming to make a lasting impact. By gaining deep insights into their audience's preferences and needs, thought leaders can create tailored content, products, and services that resonate with their target customers. This personalized approach not only enhances the overall customer experience but also positions thought leaders as innovative thinkers within their industries. Embracing audience research and client personas is a key step towards becoming a thought leader and driving success in today's competitive business landscape.

Lead Generation and Conversion

Generating leads and converting them into customers is the lifeblood of any successful organization. However, traditional lead generation techniques often fall short in capturing the attention and trust of potential customers. To stand out from the crowd, businesses are turning to thought leadership as a powerful strategy to not only attract leads but also convert them into loyal customers. In this chapter, we will explore the concept of lead generation and conversion through thought leadership, highlighting its significance and providing actionable tips to become a thought leader in your industry.

1. Defining Thought Leadership

Thought leadership refers to the practice of establishing oneself or one's organization as a trusted authority in a particular field or industry. It involves sharing valuable insights, expertise, and unique perspectives to drive meaningful conversations and shape industry trends. By positioning yourself as a thought leader, you can build credibility, gain the trust of your target audience, and ultimately, generate more leads and conversions.

2. The Role of Thought Leadership in Lead Generation

Thought leadership plays a crucial role in lead generation by creating awareness, building trust, and positioning your brand as a go-to resource. When potential customers perceive you as a thought leader, they are more likely to engage with your content, share it with others, and consider your products or services when making purchasing decisions. Additionally, thought leadership helps you attract high-quality leads who are actively seeking solutions, leading to higher conversion rates and increased customer loyalty.

3. Strategies to Become a Thought Leader

a) Identify your niche: To become a thought leader, it's essential to identify your niche and focus on a specific area where you can provide valuable insights and expertise. By narrowing your focus, you can establish yourself as an authority in that particular domain.

b) Create exceptional content: Thought leadership is built on the foundation of valuable content. Produce high-quality blog posts, articles, videos, podcasts, or whitepapers that address industry challenges, share unique perspectives, and provide practical solutions. Consistency and relevancy are key to maintaining thought leadership.

c) Leverage social media: Utilize various social media platforms to amplify your content and engage with your audience. Share your expertise, participate in industry discussions, and actively respond to comments and questions. Building a strong online presence will help you gain recognition and attract leads.

d) Collaborate and network: Establish connections with other thought leaders, industry influencers, and professionals in complementary fields. Collaborating on projects, participating in webinars or podcasts, and attending industry events can help expand your reach and enhance your thought leadership status.

e) Engage with your audience: Encourage interaction with your audience through comments, questions, and feedback. Actively engage in conversations, address concerns, and provide valuable insights. This interaction not only helps build trust but also provides valuable market insights to refine your lead generation and conversion strategies.

Summary

In the ever-evolving business landscape, thought leadership has become a powerful tool for lead generation and conversion. By establishing yourself as a trusted authority and sharing valuable insights, you can attract high-quality leads, build trust, and ultimately convert them into loyal customers. Embrace thought leadership as a long-term strategy to differentiate your brand and stay ahead of the competition in today's dynamic marketplace.

Strategies for Converting Thought Leadership Efforts into Tangible Leads

Establishing yourself as a thought leader in your industry can significantly impact your brand's visibility and credibility. Thought leadership involves positioning yourself as an expert in your field, sharing valuable insights, and providing innovative solutions to industry challenges. While building thought leadership is crucial, it is equally important to convert these efforts into tangible leads that contribute to your business growth. In this chapter, we will explore effective strategies to leverage thought leadership to generate leads and drive business success.

1. Create High-Quality Content

Thought leadership efforts begin with creating compelling and high-quality content. This content should showcase your expertise, address industry pain points, and provide valuable solutions. Use various media such as blog posts, whitepapers, videos, or podcasts to reach your target audience effectively. By consistently producing valuable content, you establish trust and credibility, which can turn readers into potential leads.

2. Optimize Content for Search Engines

To maximize the reach of your thought leadership content, it's crucial to optimize it for search engines. Conduct thorough keyword research to identify relevant keywords and incorporate them strategically into your content. By doing so, you increase the chances of your content appearing in search engine results pages, attracting organic traffic, and generating more leads.

3. Engage in Guest Blogging and Industry Publications

Collaborating with industry publications and guest blogging on reputable platforms can significantly enhance your thought leadership efforts. Identify influential publications within your niche and pitch them compelling content ideas. By leveraging their existing audience base, you can reach a wider audience and attract potential leads who are interested in your expertise.

4. Utilize Social Media Platforms

Social media platforms provide an excellent avenue to amplify your thought leadership efforts and engage with your target audience directly. Share your content across various social media channels, actively participate in industry discussions, and respond to comments and queries. By building a strong social media presence, you can attract followers, increase brand visibility, and ultimately generate leads.

5. Offer Valuable Lead Magnets

To convert your thought leadership efforts into tangible leads, offer valuable lead magnets such as e-books, webinars, or exclusive industry reports. These resources should provide valuable insights and solutions that your target audience finds irresistible. By gating these lead magnets behind a sign-up form, you can capture contact information and nurture these leads through targeted email marketing campaigns.

6. Participate in Industry Events and Webinars

Actively participating in industry events, conferences, and webinars can significantly boost your thought leadership efforts and generate leads. Speak at relevant events, host webinars, or participate in panel discussions to showcase your expertise and connect with potential leads. By engaging with a live audience, you can establish a personal connection and build trust, which can lead to tangible leads.

Summary

Building thought leadership is a valuable endeavor, but converting these efforts into tangible leads is equally important for business growth. By creating high-quality content, optimizing it for search engines, engaging in guest blogging, utilizing social media, offering valuable lead magnets, and participating in industry events, you can effectively convert your thought leadership efforts into tangible leads. Remember, consistency, authenticity, and providing valuable solutions are key to successfully leveraging thought leadership to generate leads and drive business success.

Utilizing Thought Leadership to Nurture Client Relationships Through the Sales Funnel

In today's highly competitive business landscape, establishing and nurturing strong client relationships is crucial for sustained success. One effective strategy that has gained significant traction in recent years is thought leadership. By positioning yourself or your brand as a thought leader in your industry, you can not only establish credibility but also foster trust and build long-lasting client relationships.

What is Thought Leadership?

Thought leadership refers to the practice of sharing valuable insights, expertise, and innovative ideas within your industry. It involves staying at the forefront of industry trends, continuously learning, and offering unique perspectives that can drive meaningful change. Thought leaders are seen as trusted advisors and go-to resources, making them highly influential figures within their respective fields.

Utilizing Thought Leadership in the Sales Funnel

Thought leadership can be a powerful tool in every stage of the sales funnel, from awareness to conversion and beyond. Let's explore how you can leverage thought leadership to nurture client relationships throughout the sales process:

1. Awareness Stage: Attracting Prospective Clients

Thought leadership plays a vital role in creating awareness and attracting potential clients. By consistently sharing valuable content such as blog posts, articles, videos, or podcasts, you can showcase your expertise and establish yourself as a go-to resource. This helps to create a positive first impression and piques the interest of potential clients.

2. Consideration Stage: Building Trust and Credibility

As potential clients move into the consideration stage, they seek more in-depth information and validation. This is where thought leadership can make a significant impact. By offering comprehensive whitepapers, case studies, or hosting webinars, you can provide valuable insights that address their pain points and demonstrate your expertise. This builds trust and credibility, increasing the likelihood of them choosing your products or services.

3. Decision Stage: Influencing the Buying Decision

Thought leadership can be a differentiating factor when potential clients are making their final decision. By consistently sharing industry trends, thought-provoking ideas, and success stories, you can position yourself or your brand as the obvious choice. Clients are more likely to choose a thought leader who can demonstrate a deep understanding of their challenges and offer innovative solutions.

4. Post-Sale Stage: Fostering Long-Term Relationships

Thought leadership doesn't stop after the sale is made. It is crucial to nurture client relationships even after the conversion. By continuing to share valuable insights, offering ongoing support, and staying connected through newsletters or social media, you can reinforce your position as a trusted advisor. This helps to build loyalty, encourages repeat business, and generates referrals.

Summary

Thought leadership is a powerful tool that can be utilized throughout the entire sales funnel to nurture client relationships. By consistently sharing valuable insights, establishing credibility, and building trust, you can position yourself or your brand as a trusted advisor and foster long-term client relationships. Embrace thought leadership, and watch your client relationships flourish.

Section 8

Measuring and Refining Your Thought Leadership Strategy

In the competitive business landscape, establishing oneself as a thought leader has become increasingly crucial. Thought leadership not only enhances an individual's or organization's reputation but also allows them to influence industry trends and drive innovation. However, developing an effective thought leadership strategy is just the beginning. To truly maximize its impact, measuring and refining the strategy becomes imperative. In this section, we will explore the importance of measuring thought leadership efforts and provide insights on refining your strategy for greater success.

1. Defining Thought Leadership

Before diving into measuring and refining strategies, let's briefly revisit what thought leadership entails. Thought leadership refers to the process of consistently sharing valuable insights, expertise, and unique perspectives on a particular industry or topic. It involves establishing oneself as a trusted authority and influencer, contributing to the development and advancement of the field.

2. The Importance of Measuring the Effectiveness of Thought Leadership Efforts

Measuring the effectiveness of your thought leadership efforts is essential to understand the impact you are making and identify areas for improvement. Some key reasons why measuring the effectiveness of thought leadership efforts include:

a) Tracking Reach and Engagement: Measuring metrics such as website traffic, social media engagement, and content downloads can help gauge the reach and resonance of your thought leadership content. It provides insights into which topics resonate most with your target audience, helping you tailor your strategy accordingly.

b) Evaluating Thought Leadership Impact: By analyzing metrics like media mentions, speaking opportunities, and partnership opportunities, you can assess the impact your thought leadership efforts have had on your industry. This evaluation enables you to refine your strategy to enhance your influence and expand your reach further.

c) Demonstrating ROI: Measuring thought leadership efforts allows you to demonstrate the return on investment (ROI) to stakeholders. By quantifying the results achieved through thought leadership, you can showcase the value it brings to your organization and justify the resources allocated to this strategy.

3. Key Metrics to Measure Thought Leadership Strategy

To effectively measure your thought leadership strategy, it is crucial to identify the right metrics. Here are some key metrics to consider:

a) Website Analytics: Track website traffic, time spent on pages, and conversion rates to understand the impact of your thought leadership content on your website.

b) Social Media Engagement: Monitor likes, comments, shares, and follower growth to gauge the resonance of your thought leadership content on social platforms.

c) Media Mentions: Keep track of media coverage, including interviews, articles, and quotes, to assess your visibility and influence in the industry.

d) Speaking Opportunities: Measure the number and quality of speaking invitations received to evaluate your thought leadership impact and industry recognition.

4. Refining Your Thought Leadership Strategy

Measuring your thought leadership efforts should be a continuous process, allowing you to refine your strategy for better results. Consider the following tips for refining your thought leadership strategy:

a) Analyze Data: Regularly review the metrics and data collected to identify patterns, trends, and areas for improvement. Use these insights to inform your content creation and distribution strategies.

b) Stay Current: Continuously update your knowledge and stay informed about the latest industry trends and developments. This enables you to provide timely and relevant thought leadership content.

c) Seek Feedback: Actively seek feedback from your audience, industry peers, and stakeholders. This feedback can help you understand their needs, preferences, and expectations, allowing you to refine your thought leadership strategy accordingly.

d) Collaboration and Networking: Engage with other thought leaders, industry experts, and influencers to expand your network and gain new perspectives. Collaborations can enhance your thought leadership strategy and open doors to new opportunities.

Summary

Measuring and refining your thought leadership strategy is a vital aspect of ensuring its long-term success and impact. By tracking the right metrics, analyzing data, and continuously adapting to industry trends, you can enhance your thought leadership influence, reach, and engagement. Embrace the iterative nature of thought leadership, and through consistent measurement and refinement, position yourself as a trusted authority within your industry.

Chapter 8

Key Metrics for Evaluating Thought Leadership Impact

In today's competitive business landscape, establishing thought leadership has become crucial for organizations and individuals alike. Thought leadership refers to the ability to provide valuable insights, innovative ideas, and industry expertise that positions oneself or the organization as a trusted authority in a particular field. However, measuring the impact of thought leadership efforts can be challenging. In this chapter, we will explore the key metrics that can help evaluate the effectiveness and impact of thought leadership initiatives.

1. Website Traffic

One of the primary metrics to consider when evaluating thought leadership impact is website traffic. Increased traffic indicates that your thought leadership content is attracting and engaging the target audience. Analyzing the number of unique visitors, page views, and average time spent on the site can provide insights into the level of interest generated by your thought leadership content.

2. Social Media Engagement

Social media platforms play a vital role in thought leadership dissemination. Monitoring metrics such as likes, shares, comments, and followers on platforms like LinkedIn, Twitter, or Facebook can gauge the impact of your thought leadership content. High engagement suggests that your ideas resonate with the audience and that they find value in your insights.

3. Content Downloads

If you offer downloadable content such as whitepapers, reports, or e-books, tracking the number of downloads can provide valuable insights. This metric helps determine the level of interest and the perceived value of your thought leadership content. It also allows you to identify which topics resonate the most with your target audience.

4. Media Mentions and Press Coverage

Thought leaders often attract attention from industry publications, media outlets, and journalists. Monitoring media mentions and press coverage can help evaluate the reach and impact of your thought leadership. This metric demonstrates how your ideas are being recognized and shared by influential sources, further establishing your credibility and authority in the industry.

5. Speaking Engagements and Webinars

Thought leaders are often invited to speak at conferences, webinars, and industry events. Tracking the number of speaking engagements and webinar registrations can indicate the level of demand for your expertise. Additionally, evaluating attendee feedback, session ratings, and post-event surveys can provide insights into the impact of your thought leadership presentations.

6. Lead Generation and Conversion Rates:

Effective thought leadership content can generate leads and contribute to conversions. Monitoring the number of leads generated from thought leadership initiatives and analyzing the conversion rates can help evaluate the impact on the overall sales funnel. By tracking the origin of leads and analyzing their quality, you can determine the effectiveness of your thought leadership in driving business growth.

Summary

Measuring the impact of thought leadership is essential to understand the effectiveness of your efforts and make informed decisions for future strategies. By analyzing key metrics such as website traffic, social media engagement, content downloads, media mentions, speaking engagements, and lead generation, you can assess the reach, influence, and value of your thought leadership initiatives. Remember, thought leadership is an ongoing process, and regularly evaluating these metrics will help refine your approach and establish a strong position in your industry.

Analyzing and Adapting Content Strategies

Content strategies play a crucial role in helping businesses establish a strong online presence and engage with their target audience effectively. However, simply creating content without thoughtful analysis and adaptation can limit its impact and hinder long-term success. To truly excel in the realm of content marketing, thought leadership becomes a key aspect of this process. In this chapter, we will delve into the importance of analyzing and adapting content strategies, highlighting how thought leadership can enhance these efforts.

Analyzing Content Strategies

Effective content strategies begin with a thorough analysis of the current landscape. By examining market trends, competitor approaches, and customer preferences, businesses can gain valuable insights that inform their content creation process. This analysis helps identify gaps and opportunities, ensuring that the content produced aligns with the needs and interests of the target audience.

Keyword research plays a vital role in content analysis. By identifying relevant keywords and incorporating them strategically into content, businesses can optimize their search engine rankings and increase visibility. This analysis also helps in understanding the language customers use, enabling businesses to tailor their content accordingly.

Adapting Content Strategies

While analysis sets the foundation, adapting content strategies is crucial to remain relevant and responsive. As the digital landscape evolves, businesses must continually refine and adapt their content to meet changing customer demands. By monitoring key performance indicators (KPIs) such as engagement rates, click-throughs, and conversions, businesses can gauge the effectiveness of their content and identify areas for improvement.

Thought Leadership in Content Strategies

Thought leadership is a concept that has gained significant traction in recent years. It involves positioning oneself or a business as an industry expert, providing valuable insights and innovative ideas to the target audience. By becoming a thought leader, businesses can establish credibility and build trust, which ultimately leads to increased customer loyalty and brand recognition. Thought leadership can be integrated into content strategies in several ways.

Firstly, by conducting in-depth research and analysis, businesses can uncover unique insights and perspectives that set them apart from competitors. Sharing these insights through thought-provoking blog posts, whitepapers, or videos can establish the business as a trusted authority in their industry.

Secondly, thought leadership can be demonstrated through content curation and sharing. By curating relevant and valuable content from various sources and adding insightful commentary, businesses can position themselves as a go-to resource for industry-related information. This approach not only provides value to the audience but also showcases the business's expertise and commitment to staying up-to-date with the latest trends.

Lastly, actively engaging with the audience through social media platforms and online communities allows businesses to foster meaningful conversations and build relationships. By responding to comments, addressing queries, and participating in industry discussions, businesses can establish themselves as thought leaders who genuinely care about their audience's needs.

Summary

Analyzing and adapting content strategies are essential for businesses aiming to thrive in the digital landscape. By incorporating thought leadership into these strategies, businesses can differentiate themselves, build credibility, and establish long-lasting relationships with their audience. Through thorough analysis, adaptation, and the display of expertise, businesses can elevate their content strategies to new heights of success.

Continuous Improvement and Growth

Businesses and individuals alike are constantly seeking ways to stay ahead of the curve. Continuous improvement and growth have become essential components of success, and thought leadership plays a pivotal role in this journey. By harnessing the power of thought leadership, organizations can foster innovation, drive change, and propel themselves towards sustainable growth. In this chapter, we will explore how continuous improvement and growth can be achieved through the lens of thought leadership.

1. Defining Continuous Improvement

Continuous improvement is a mindset that revolves around constantly refining processes, products, and strategies to enhance performance and achieve better outcomes. Thought leadership, as a concept, refers to individuals or organizations that are recognized as experts and innovators in their respective fields. Combining these two elements creates a powerful force that drives progress and fosters growth.

2. The Role of Thought Leadership in Continuous Improvement

Thought leaders are at the forefront of change, challenging conventional wisdom and pushing boundaries. By sharing their expertise, insights, and experiences, they inspire others to adopt a similar mindset of continuous improvement. Thought leadership encourages individuals and organizations to question the status quo, embrace new ideas, and actively seek opportunities for growth.

3. Sharing Best Practices and Knowledge

Thought leaders serve as catalysts for growth by sharing best practices and knowledge gained through their experiences. Through blogs, articles, and public speaking engagements, they disseminate valuable insights, lessons learned, and innovative approaches. By tapping into this extensive pool of wisdom, individuals and organizations can gain a competitive edge and accelerate their growth trajectory.

4. Fostering a Culture of Learning

Continuous improvement and growth thrive in environments that foster a culture of learning. Thought leaders emphasize the importance of ongoing education, both for personal and professional development. By encouraging employees to expand their knowledge, acquire new skills, and embrace a growth mindset, organizations can create a workforce that is adaptable, innovative, and constantly striving for improvement.

5. Embracing Innovation

Thought leadership and continuous improvement go hand in hand with innovation. Thought leaders challenge the status quo, identify gaps, and propose innovative solutions. By encouraging a culture of innovation within organizations, they inspire employees to think creatively, embrace change, and contribute to the continuous improvement process. Innovation becomes a driving force behind growth and a key differentiator in today's competitive landscape.

Summary

Continuous improvement and growth are critical for individuals and organizations seeking long-term success. By leveraging the power of thought leadership, we can tap into a wealth of knowledge, foster a culture of learning, and drive innovation. Thought leaders inspire us to challenge the norms, embrace change, and constantly seek ways to improve. Embracing continuous improvement and growth through thought leadership allows us to unlock our full potential and thrive in an ever-evolving world.

Section 9

Case Studies and Success Stories

Organizations are constantly seeking innovative solutions and strategies to achieve success. One powerful tool that can help businesses gain a competitive edge is the use of case studies and success stories. In this section, we will explore the significance of case studies and success stories from a thought leadership perspective, shedding light on how these tools can provide valuable insights and inspire others to achieve greatness.

1. Understanding Thought Leadership

Thought leadership refers to the ability to influence and inspire others through the demonstration of expertise and innovative thinking. By sharing valuable knowledge and insights, thought leaders position themselves as experts in their respective fields. Case studies and success stories, when presented in a thoughtful and analytical manner, can serve as powerful thought leadership tools.

2. Leveraging Case Studies

Case studies provide an in-depth analysis of a particular situation, problem, or project, highlighting the challenges faced and the strategies implemented to overcome them. By presenting real-life examples, case studies demonstrate how businesses have addressed complex issues and achieved success. Thought leaders can leverage case studies to showcase their expertise and offer valuable insights to their audience.

3. Extracting Key Lessons

Case studies allow thought leaders to extract key lessons from successful endeavors. By analyzing the strategies, decisions, and actions that led to success, thought leaders can distill valuable knowledge that can be applied to similar situations. This process of extracting lessons not only demonstrates thought leadership but also provides a roadmap for others to follow in their own endeavors.

4. Inspiring Success Stories

Success stories are narratives that highlight the achievements and triumphs of individuals, organizations, or even communities. These stories inspire and motivate others by showcasing the journey from challenges and setbacks to remarkable achievements. Thought leaders can use success stories to inspire their audience, offering a source of motivation and encouragement to strive for greatness.

5. Sharing Insights and Expertise

Thought leaders can use case studies and success stories to share their insights and expertise with their audience. By presenting these real-life examples, thought leaders can demonstrate their understanding of complex problems, innovative thinking, and the ability to deliver results. This sharing of knowledge not only establishes thought leaders as experts but also fosters a sense of trust and credibility among their audience.

Summary

Case studies and success stories are invaluable tools that can elevate thought leadership efforts. By leveraging these tools, thought leaders can showcase their expertise, provide valuable insights, and inspire others to achieve greatness. Whether through the analysis of case studies or the presentation of success stories, thought leaders have the ability to influence and shape the perspectives of their audience, ultimately contributing to the growth and success of individuals and organizations alike.

Chapter 9

Real-world Examples of Effective Thought Leadership Strategies

Thought leadership has become an essential aspect of any successful business or individual looking to establish themselves as an authority in their field. By providing valuable insights, innovative ideas, and industry expertise, thought leaders can shape conversations, influence opinions, and drive meaningful change. In this chapter, we will explore some real-world examples of effective thought leadership strategies, highlighting how these individuals or organizations have utilized their expertise to make a significant impact.

1. Elon Musk: Revolutionizing the Electric Vehicle Industry

Elon Musk, CEO of Tesla and SpaceX, is widely regarded as a thought leader in the electric vehicle (EV) industry. Through his visionary ideas and relentless pursuit of innovation, Musk has successfully positioned himself as a leading authority on sustainable transportation. By promoting the benefits of EVs, sharing his knowledge on battery technology, and challenging traditional automotive industry norms, Musk has not only transformed the perception of electric vehicles but also influenced global conversations on climate change and the future of transportation.

2. Sheryl Sandberg: Empowering Women in the Workplace

Sheryl Sandberg, the Chief Operating Officer of Facebook, has emerged as a prominent thought leader in advocating for gender equality and women's empowerment in the workplace. Through her book "Lean In" and various speaking engagements, Sandberg has offered practical advice and strategies for women to overcome barriers and achieve their professional goals. By sharing her personal experiences and highlighting the systemic challenges women face, Sandberg has inspired a global movement and sparked conversations on the importance of diversity and inclusion in corporate settings.

3. Simon Sinek: Inspiring Leadership and Purpose-driven Organizations

Simon Sinek, a renowned author and speaker, has become a thought leader in the realm of leadership and organizational culture. His TED Talk, "How Great Leaders Inspire Action," has garnered millions of views and has been instrumental in shaping discussions around effective leadership. Sinek emphasizes the significance of starting with why, inspiring individuals to align their actions with a clear purpose. By sharing his insights on leadership and encouraging organizations to adopt a purpose-driven approach, Sinek has influenced countless leaders and helped shape a new paradigm for successful and impactful businesses.

4. Patagonia: Leading the Way in Sustainable Business Practices

Patagonia, an outdoor clothing and gear company, has established itself as a thought leader in the realm of sustainable business practices. Through its mission of "building the best product, causing no unnecessary harm, and using business to inspire and implement solutions to the environmental crisis," Patagonia has become a role model for other companies. By transparently sharing their sustainability efforts, including initiatives like the "Worn Wear" program and their commitment to fair trade, Patagonia has not only built a loyal customer base but has also influenced the industry to prioritize environmental responsibility.

Summary

These real-world examples demonstrate the power of thought leadership strategies in driving positive change and influencing industry conversations. Elon Musk, Sheryl Sandberg, Simon Sinek, and Patagonia have leveraged their expertise, passion, and innovative ideas to become thought leaders in their respective fields. By sharing their insights, challenging the status quo, and inspiring others, these individuals and organizations have made a lasting impact on their industries and society as a whole. Embracing thought leadership can be a powerful tool for anyone looking to establish themselves as an authority and drive meaningful change in their fields.

Lessons Learned and Insights Gained

It is essential to constantly learn, adapt, and gain insights to stay ahead of the curve. As thought leaders, we understand the value of continuous growth and the importance of sharing our experiences to inspire and educate others. In this chapter, we delve into the lessons learned and insights gained, exploring various aspects of thought leadership. Through our reflections, we aim to offer valuable takeaways and provoke insightful discussions. Join us on this journey of knowledge and enlightenment.

1. Nurturing Innovation: Unlocking the Power of Creativity

Let's now we explore the significance of nurturing innovation and unlocking the power of creativity. We discuss the lessons we have learned from our experiences as thought leaders, shedding light on how embracing innovation can drive success. We delve into the importance of fostering a culture that encourages creativity, sharing insights on how to inspire and empower individuals to think outside the box. Through real-life examples and case studies, we demonstrate the impact of innovative thinking on thought leadership.

2. Embracing Change: Adapting and Thriving in a Dynamic Environment

Change is inevitable, and as thought leaders, we understand the importance of embracing it. We share the lessons we learned from navigating through dynamic environments and adapting to new circumstances. We discuss the challenges we faced, the insights gained, and the strategies we employed to thrive amidst change. From technological advancements to shifting market trends, we delve into how embracing change can be a catalyst for thought leadership success.

3. Building Meaningful Relationships: The Power of Networking

Thought leadership is not just about knowledge and expertise; it also relies on building meaningful relationships. We explore the lessons we have learned about the power of networking and relationship-building. We delve into the insights gained from connecting with like-minded individuals, industry experts, and potential collaborators. Through personal anecdotes and practical tips, we share strategies for effective networking and highlight its impact on thought leadership growth.

4. Overcoming Challenges: Lessons in Resilience and Perseverance

No journey is without its challenges, and as thought leaders, we have faced our fair share. We reflect on the lessons learned from overcoming obstacles and the insights gained from persevering through adversity. We discuss the importance of resilience, sharing personal stories and strategies for bouncing back from setbacks. By exploring the challenges we encountered and the lessons we learned, we aim to inspire others to embrace resilience in their own thought leadership journeys.

Summary

We have delved into various aspects of thought leadership, sharing our lessons learned and insights gained. From nurturing innovation and embracing change to building meaningful relationships and overcoming challenges, we have explored the key elements that contribute to thought leadership success. By applying these thought leadership keywords, we hope to inspire and empower others to embark on their own journeys of growth and enlightenment. Remember, thought leadership is not just about what we know, but how we share our knowledge and inspire others along the way.

Section 10

The Future of Thought Leadership

In today's rapidly evolving world, where information is readily available at our fingertips, thought leadership has emerged as a crucial concept. It refers to individuals or organizations that are recognized as experts in their respective fields, possessing deep knowledge and insights that shape industry trends and influence others. However, as we move forward, the future of thought leadership is poised for a transformation that will redefine its impact and significance. Let's explore the key trends and potential developments that will shape the future of thought leadership.

1. Digital Transformation

The digital revolution has fundamentally changed the way we consume and share information. In the future, thought leadership will increasingly rely on digital platforms to disseminate ideas and insights to a global audience. With the rise of social media, podcasts, videos, and other digital media, thought leaders will have greater opportunities to connect with their target audience, build communities, and establish themselves as trusted authorities.

2. Personalization and Niche Expertise

As the digital landscape becomes increasingly crowded, standing out as a thought leader will require a focus on personalization and niche expertise. Thought leaders will need to identify their unique value proposition and cater to specific target audiences, offering tailored insights and solutions. This personalization will enable thought leaders to establish stronger connections and foster more meaningful engagements with their followers.

3. Collaboration and Co-Creation

In the future, thought leadership will move away from a solitary endeavor towards collaboration and co-creation. Building partnerships and alliances with other thought leaders or organizations will become essential for amplifying influence and reaching a wider audience.

By combining expertise and perspectives, thought leaders can create more comprehensive and innovative solutions to complex challenges, driving meaningful change in their industries.

4. Embracing Diversity and Inclusion

As thought leadership evolves, there will be a growing emphasis on diversity and inclusion. Recognizing the value of diverse perspectives and experiences, thought leaders will actively seek out voices from underrepresented groups. By embracing diversity, thought leadership will become more inclusive, leading to richer discussions, broader insights, and a more equitable representation of ideas.

5. Ethical Leadership and Responsibility

The future of thought leadership will demand a greater focus on ethical leadership and responsibility. Thought leaders will be expected to uphold high ethical standards and promote values such as transparency, authenticity, and social responsibility. As society becomes more conscious of the impact of thought leaders, their influence will be closely scrutinized, necessitating a commitment to ethical practices and accountability.

Summary

The future of thought leadership holds immense potential for growth and transformation. With the digital revolution, personalization, collaboration, diversity, and ethical leadership at the forefront, thought leaders will have the opportunity to shape industries, inspire change, and create a positive impact. By embracing these key trends and adapting to the evolving landscape, thought leaders can continue to be a driving force in shaping the future of their respective fields.

Chapter 10

Predictions and Trends

In the future, staying ahead of the curve is crucial for businesses and individuals alike. The ability to foresee upcoming trends and make accurate predictions is a valuable skill that can shape the success of any endeavor. As thought leaders, we understand the significance of staying informed and providing insightful perspectives on the future. We therefore, delve into the realm of predictions and trends, offering our expertise and thought leadership to guide you through the ever-changing landscape.

1. Embracing Disruption: Predicting Industry Transformations

We explore how industries are being disrupted and transformed by emerging technologies and changing consumer behaviors. Our thought leadership sheds light on the potential impact of these disruptions and offers predictions on how businesses can adapt and thrive in the face of such challenges. From the rise of artificial intelligence to the growing influence of the sharing economy, we analyze the trends that are reshaping entire industries and provide actionable insights for staying ahead.

2. Future of Work: Predicting the Workforce of Tomorrow

As automation and artificial intelligence continue to reshape the workplace, predicting the future of work has become a critical topic. We share our thought leadership on the evolving dynamics of employment, the gig economy, and the skills that will be in high demand in the future. By analyzing the trends in remote work, flexible schedules, and digital collaboration, we offer predictions on how the workforce will evolve and how organizations can prepare for the changing landscape.

3. Consumer Behavior: Predicting the Next Big Thing

Understanding consumer behavior is essential for businesses to stay relevant and competitive. We leverage our thought leadership to predict the emerging trends that will shape consumer preferences and purchasing habits. From the influence of social media to the rise of sustainability, we analyze the factors that drive consumer decision-making and offer valuable insights into how businesses can adapt their strategies to meet evolving consumer demands.

4. Technology and Innovation: Predicting the Next Breakthrough

Technological advancements continue to disrupt industries and create new opportunities. We explore the latest developments in technology and innovation, offering our thought leadership on the potential breakthroughs that will shape the future. From blockchain to virtual reality, we predict the trends that will revolutionize various sectors and provide guidance on how organizations can leverage these advancements to gain a competitive edge.

5. Global Trends: Predicting the Future of the World

The world is interconnected, and global trends have a profound impact on businesses and societies. In this section, we analyze geopolitical, economic, and environmental trends that will shape the future. Our thought leadership offers predictions on the potential consequences of these trends and provides insights into how organizations can navigate the complexities of a rapidly changing world.

Summary

As thought leaders in the field, we are committed to providing you with valuable insights and predictions to help you navigate the uncertainties of the future. Through our analysis and thought leadership, we aim to empower you to make informed decisions and stay ahead of the trends that will shape your industry. Join us in this exciting journey of exploring predictions and trends, and let us guide you towards a successful future.

Sustaining Thought Leadership Impact

In today's fast-paced evolving world, thought leadership has emerged as a crucial aspect of success for individuals and organizations alike. Being recognized as a thought leader in your field not only establishes you as an authority but also enables you to influence and shape the direction of your industry. However, sustaining thought leadership impact requires continuous effort and strategic planning. In this chapter, we will explore the key strategies and actions necessary to maintain and enhance your thought leadership position.

1. Consistent Knowledge Sharing

Thought leadership is built on the foundation of sharing valuable insights and knowledge with your audience. To sustain your impact, it is essential to consistently create and distribute high-quality content. This includes writing blog posts, articles, whitepapers, or even publishing research findings. By regularly sharing your expertise, you position yourself as a reliable source of information, keeping your audience engaged and informed.

2. Engage in Collaborative Networking

Collaboration with other thought leaders in your field can significantly amplify your impact. Actively seek opportunities to engage in joint projects, participate in panel discussions, or contribute to industry-specific events. By forging connections with like-minded individuals, you expand your reach and gain access to new audiences. Collaborative networking also provide valuable opportunities for knowledge exchange and learning from peers, further enhancing your thought leadership position.

3. Embrace Thought Leadership Platforms

In this digital age, thought leadership platforms such as social media, podcasts, and webinars have become powerful tools for sustaining impact. Utilize these platforms to share your insights, engage with your audience, and establish yourself as a thought leader.

Regularly contribute to discussions, answer questions, and participate in relevant industry conversations. By actively participating in these platforms, you ensure your voice is heard and your impact is prolonged.

4. Foster Innovation and Adaptation

Thought leadership is not stagnant; it requires continuous innovation and adaptation to stay relevant. Stay updated with the latest industry trends, technological advancements, and emerging practices. Being at the forefront of change enables you to provide valuable insights and solutions to your audience. Embrace new technologies, experiment with different formats of content, and adapt your strategies to meet the evolving needs of your industry.

5. Cultivate a Strong Personal Brand

A strong personal brand is an essential element of sustaining thought leadership impact. Consistently deliver value through your content, communicate your unique perspective, and establish your expertise in your niche. Craft a compelling personal brand story that resonates with your audience, effectively differentiating yourself from others in your field. By consistently reinforcing your personal brand, you maintain and enhance your thought leadership impact.

Summary

Sustaining thought leadership impact requires a proactive and continuous effort. By consistently sharing knowledge, engaging in collaborative networking, utilizing thought leadership platforms, fostering innovation, and cultivating a strong personal brand, you can ensure your influence and impact endure. Remember, thought leadership is not just about being recognized as an authority; it is about making a meaningful and lasting contribution to your industry.

Section 11

Recap of Key Points:

In this section, we will recap the key points discussed so far regarding thought leadership. Thought leadership refers to the ability of an individual or organization to establish themselves as a trusted authority in a specific field or industry. It involves sharing valuable insights, knowledge, and expertise to influence and inspire others.

1.   Establishing Credibility

Thought leadership requires building a reputation for expertise and credibility in a particular domain. This can be achieved through consistently providing high-quality content, research, and unique perspectives that offer solutions to industry challenges.

2. Building Trust

Thought leaders are trusted sources of information and guidance. By consistently delivering valuable and reliable content, thought leaders can gain the trust of their audience, which is crucial for their influence and impact.

3. Creating Influence

Thought leadership allows individuals or organizations to shape industry conversations and trends. By sharing innovative ideas, thought leaders can influence the way others think, make decisions, and take action.

4. Driving Engagement

Thought leaders actively engage with their audience through various channels, such as blogs, social media, webinars, conferences, and podcasts. This engagement fosters a sense of community and encourages discussions, collaborations, and knowledge sharing.

5. Fostering Growth

Thought leadership not only benefits the individual or organization but also contributes to the growth of the industry as a whole. By sharing insights, best practices, and thought-provoking ideas, thought leaders can drive innovation, inspire others, and contribute to the overall advancement of their field.

Final Thoughts on the Power of Thought Leadership

Thought leadership has proven to be a powerful tool in today's dynamic and competitive business landscape. By establishing oneself as a trusted authority, thought leaders can enhance their personal brand, attract new opportunities, and influence industry direction.

The impact of thought leadership extends beyond personal gains. It creates a ripple effect, inspiring others to excel, innovate, and contribute to the collective growth of the industry. Thought leaders have the power to shape conversations, challenge conventional wisdom, and drive positive change.

However, thought leadership is not built overnight. It requires consistent effort, dedication, and a genuine commitment to adding value to the industry. It is crucial to stay updated with the latest trends, research, and developments to remain relevant and maintain credibility.

Thought leadership is a powerful concept that can transform individuals and organizations into influential industry leaders. By leveraging their knowledge, expertise, and unique perspectives, thought leaders can drive innovation, inspire others, and make a significant impact in their fields. Embracing thought leadership can open doors to new opportunities, foster growth, and leave a lasting legacy in the industry.

Chapter 11

Unlocking Thought Leadership: Essential Resources and Insights

In today's fast-paced world, establishing oneself as a thought leader is crucial for professional growth and influence. Thought leadership entails sharing innovative ideas, unique perspectives, and expert knowledge to shape industries and inspire others. To assist you in your journey towards becoming a thought leader, this chapter provides valuable resources, recommended tools, further reading suggestions, and information about the author.

1. Resources for Thought Leadership

Thought leadership requires a constant pursuit of knowledge and staying up-to-date with the latest trends. Here are some essential resources to help you enhance your thought leadership skills:

a) Industry-specific publications and journals: Subscribe to reputable publications in your industry to gain insights into emerging trends, research findings, and expert opinions. Stay informed and leverage this knowledge to contribute to meaningful conversations.

b) Webinars and podcasts: Engage with thought leaders through webinars and podcasts that cover topics relevant to your field. These platforms offer valuable insights, interviews, and discussions, enabling you to learn from established thought leaders.

c) Professional networking and Community Building: Join online forums, industry-specific groups, and social media communities to connect with like-minded professionals. Engaging in discussions, sharing your expertise, and learning from others will help you refine your thought leadership skills.

2. Recommended Tools for Thought Leadership: To effectively share your ideas and amplify your thought leadership, consider these tools:

a) Blogging platforms: Start your own blog to share your unique insights, experiences, and expertise. Platforms like WordPress, Medium, or Blogger offer user-friendly interfaces and help you reach a wider audience.

b) Social media platforms: Leverage social media channels such as LinkedIn, Twitter, and Instagram to share your thought leadership content, engage with your audience, and connect with other thought leaders. These platforms provide an excellent opportunity to build your personal brand and expand your network.

c) Content creation tools: Utilize tools like Canva for creating visually appealing graphics, Grammarly for enhancing your writing, and Hootsuite for scheduling and managing your social media posts. These tools streamline your content creation process and ensure your thought leadership materials are professional and error-free.

3. Further Reading and References:

Expand your knowledge and deepen your thought leadership skills by exploring the following resources:

a) Books: Read influential books on thought leadership, personal branding, and industry-specific topics. Some recommended titles include "The Content Trap" by Bharat Anand, "The Innovator's Dilemma" by Clayton M. Christensen, and "The Lean Startup" by Eric Ries.

b) Research papers and case studies: Dive into research papers, academic journals, and case studies to gain insights into successful thought leadership strategies and examples. Publications like Harvard Business Review, McKinsey Quarterly, and MIT Sloan Management Review offer valuable research-based articles.

c) Online courses and webinars: Enroll in online courses or attend webinars focused on thought leadership, personal branding, or public speaking. Platforms like Coursera, Udemy, and TED Talks often feature courses and presentations by renowned thought leaders.

.

Summary

Becoming a thought leader requires continuous learning, leveraging valuable resources, and utilizing the right tools. By exploring the recommended resources, tools, and further reading suggestions mentioned above, you can enhance your thought leadership journey and make a significant impact in your industry. Embrace the power of thought leadership, share your unique perspectives, and inspire others to drive meaningful change.

.

About the Author – Adebola Adeola MBA (Leicester) UK

The author of "Unlocking the Power of Thought Leadership to Acquire New Clients" holds an esteemed Master's in Business Administration (MBA) from the University of Leicester, UK. This academic foundation serves as a solid framework for his multifaceted career in the realms of Strategic Leadership, Marketing, Advertising, Public relations, and Digital Marketing.

Professional Expertise

With over four decades of experience, the author has honed his expertise in various domains within advertising and corporate communications. He possesses a comprehensive understanding of both the agency and client sides of the industry, providing a holistic view of the marketing, advertising and public relations landscape.

Industry Experience

Having traversed the dynamic landscape of advertising agencies and corporate communications, the author brings a wealth of practical knowledge. His extensive tenure in managing corporate communications on the client side has cultivated an acute understanding of strategic messaging, brand positioning, and audience engagement.

CEO of Digital Marketing Services:

As a CEO in the digital marketing realm, the author has demonstrated exemplary leadership in steering digital marketing services to success. Their leadership encompasses a wide array of specialized areas, showcasing a profound grasp of the digital sphere.

Specialized Domains

The author's expertise extends across an impressive array of specialized areas, including but not limited to:

Competitive Advertising Intelligence: Proficiency in analyzing and leveraging competitive advertising strategies to gain market advantage.

Programmatic Advertising: Mastery in leveraging automated processes for targeted and efficient advertising campaigns.

Financial PR: Expertise in navigating the intersection of finance and public relations, ensuring effective communication in financial contexts.

Lead Marketing: Strategic implementation of lead generation tactics to drive business growth.

Content Copywriting: Crafting compelling and impactful content that resonates with target audiences.

Social Media Marketing: Harnessing the power of social media platforms for brand visibility, engagement, and conversion.

Web Development and Design: A keen eye for designing and developing engaging, user-friendly websites.

SEO Marketing: Profound knowledge of search engine optimization techniques to enhance online visibility and rankings.

Email Nurturing Sequencing: Creating effective email nurturing campaigns for lead conversion and customer retention.

Contributions to Thought Leadership

The book titled "Unlocking the Power of Thought Leadership to Acquire New Clients," is authored by an industry luminary in corporate communications and signified his commitment to sharing valuable insights and strategies to the ever-changing industry dynamics. The book serves as a comprehensive guide for professionals seeking to leverage thought leadership as a catalyst for acquiring new clients, drawing from the author's extensive experience and expertise.

Summary

The author's rich blend of academic prowess, hands-on industry experience, and visionary leadership in the digital marketing landscape underscores his authority in the field. Through his book and professional accomplishments, he continues to shape and inspire the industry, empowering others to navigate the evolving landscape of digital marketing for client acquisition through the power of thought leadership.

.